THE MAKING OF
ENGLISH TEACHERS

Open University Press

English, Language, and Education series

General Editor: Anthony Adams

Lecturer in Education, University of Cambridge

TITLES IN THE SERIES

Narrative and Argument
Richard Andrews (ed.)

The Problem with Poetry
Richard Andrews

Writing Development
Roslyn Arnold

Writing Policy in Action
Eve Bearne and Cath Farrow

Time for Drama
Roma Burgess and Pamela Gaudry

Readers, Texts, Teachers
Bill Corcoran and Emrys Evans (eds.)

Thinking Through English
Paddy Creber

Developing Response to Poetry
Patrick Dias and Michael Hayhoe

Developing English
Peter Dougill (ed.)

The Primary Language Book
Peter Dougill and Richard Knott

Children Talk About Books
Donald Fry

Literary Theory and English Teaching
Peter Griffith

Lesbian and Gay Issues in the English Classroom
Simon Harris

Reading and Response
Mike Hayhoe and Stephen Parker (eds.)

Assessing English
Brian Johnston

Lipservice: The Story of Talk in Schools
Pat Jones

The English Department in a Changing World
Richard Knott

Oracy Matters
Margaret MacLure, Terry Phillips and Andrew Wilkinson (eds.)

Language Awareness for Teachers
Bill Mittins

Beginning Writing
John Nichols *et al.*

Teaching Literature for Examinations
Robert Protherough

Developing Response to Fiction
Robert Protherough

The Making of English Teachers
Robert Protherough and Judith Atkinson

Microcomputers and the Language Arts
Brent Robinson

Young People Reading
Charles Sarland

English Teaching from A–Z
Wayne Sawyer, Anthony Adams and Ken Watson

Reconstructing 'A' Level English
Patrick Scott

School Writing
Yanina Sheeran and Douglas Barnes

Reading Narrative as Literature
Andrew Stibbs

Collaboration and Writing
Morag Styles (ed.)

Reading Within and Beyond the Classroom
Dan Taverner

Reading for Real
Barrie Wade (ed.)

English Teaching in Perspective
Ken Watson

The Quality of Writing
Andrew Wilkinson

The Writing of Writing
Andrew Wilkinson (ed.)

Spoken English Illuminated
Andrew Wilkinson, Alan Davies and Deborah Berrill

THE MAKING OF ENGLISH TEACHERS

Robert Protherough and Judith Atkinson

Open University Press
Milton Keynes · Philadelphia

Open University Press
Celtic Court
22 Ballmoor
Buckingham
MK18 1XW

and
1900 Frost Road, Suite 101
Bristol, PA 19007, USA

First Published 1991

British Library Cataloguing-in-Publication Data

Protherough, Robert
   The making of English teachers. – (English,
   language, and education series)
   I. Title   II. Atkinson, Judith   III. Series
   420.7

   ISBN 0–335–09374–4

Library of Congress Cataloging-in-Publication Data

Protherough, Robert.
    The making of English teachers/by Robert Protherough and Judith
Atkinson.
        p.   cm. – (English, language, and education series)
    Includes bibliographical references and index.
    ISBN 0–335–09374–4
    1. English teachers – Training of.   2. English philology – Study and
teaching (Higher)   I. Atkinson, Judith.   II. Title.   III. Series.
PE66.P76   1991
420′. 7 – dc20   91–17907
                                                                      CIP

Typeset by Graphicraft Typesetters Ltd., Hong Kong
Printed in Great Britain by Biddles Ltd., Guildford and Kings Lynn

Dedicated to all those English teachers whose practice, conversation and writings have helped to make us — and this volume.

Contents

Acknowledgements

We are very grateful that, despite extreme pressure in a period of rapid change, so many teachers, advisers and lecturers found time to help us with the enquiry that provides much of the material for this book. It was particularly encouraging that many of them also wrote letters to assure us that they shared our concern and provided additional supporting materials. We hope that this book, in which so many of their words are quoted, may be some return for these efforts.

We are also indebted to Anthony Adams (Cambridge University), Chris Davies and Peter Benton (Oxford University), Colin Peacock (Stirling University) and Eric Hadley (South Glamorgan Institute of Higher Education), the authors of the four chapters that give specific examples of current teacher education programmes and the principles on which they are based. By describing work of different kinds, post-graduate and concurrent, in university and public sector institutions in England, Wales and Scotland, they combine to give a vivid picture of the variety of effective practice that we hope to see maintained.

Our final debt is to the editor of this series, Anthony Adams, who was instrumental in suggesting the need for a book about teacher education in English and who encouraged our work throughout (not least by writing one of the chapters). We share his hope that this will be a significant contribution to the current debate.

Robert Protherough
and Judith Atkinson

General editor's introduction

Given the widespread recent discussion about patterns for initial teacher education it is surprising how little has concentrated upon the preparation prospective teachers receive for the subjects for which they will be responsible. It is all too often assumed, especially in the case of teachers intending to teach in secondary schools, that all they need will be a degree in the subject and that the rest is simply a matter of learning some skills of classroom management. At its most extreme this view argues for an apprenticeship model of training, learning on the job from an experienced 'master-teacher'. No one would deny the importance of classroom practice in initial teacher education, yet it should also be clear that more is needed than this. There is, after all, as evidenced by this series, a large theoretical body of ideas about the teaching of English with which it would be unrealistic to expect all classroom teachers to be equally familiar. In any case there is no particular reason why university courses in English, themselves enormously varied in their content, should be seen as leading to a career in teaching. Much that they quite rightly contain at university level will prove largely irrelevant in most school classrooms; other areas with which teachers of English need to be familiar, the whole field of children's literature for example, are unlikely to be covered in most university courses.

This is probably more true of English than other school subjects, a product of the universal requirement of English in the curriculum and the highly personal nature of much of the teaching involved. In the survey which Protherough and Atkinson cite in these pages of the attitudes of English teachers to their art it is clear that English teachers see themselves as in many ways different from teachers of other school subjects. This view might of course be replicated by teachers in other subject areas. If so, it would make the argument of this book even more important. We cannot dissociate the processes of teacher education from the personal development and continuing education of the potential teacher, nor can we divorce such concerns from those based upon the nature of the subject itself.

We need, in consequence, more studies of this kind dealing with subjects other than English. It would be interesting to contrast the findings from the Protherough and Atkinson survey with similar surveys conducted with, say, modern languages or music teachers. It is surprising how little research has been done in this area and how much we are reliant on hearsay and anecdotal evidence for our information about what actually goes on in teacher education courses.

The four case studies which this book contains, one of which I have myself contributed, do provide a useful 'snapshot' of particular institutions in action and, in themselves, demonstrate that, within the diversity of traditions they represent, there are nonetheless a number of common concerns which they share. They typically deal with current concerns which could well have changed or developed by the time this book is published. My own contribution, for example, deals with very different issues from those that were uppermost the last time that I wrote on this matter.

The value of the case studies is their concrete encapsulation of the more general issues with which the major portion of the book is concerned. In these chapters by the two editors very important questions are addressed both histori- cally and practically. These include attempts to define what is special about English teaching, to describe the qualities that underlie good English teachers, to relate issues to do with the preparation for the English classroom to the more general and wider debate on teacher education, and to provide some guidelines for the future.

What emerges from these pages is a constant concern for both quality and clarity of purpose. The volume should be of interest not only to initial teacher educators (which group must include the teachers who work with them in the schools as well as those in the training institutions), to the students themselves as a means of providing a focus for an audit of their courses, and for all those concerned to make our schools better and more humane institutions. In the pres- ent climate in England and Wales this ought to include governors of schools as well as those who teach in them.

Writing about teacher education is an activity that takes place in a highly charged and politicized atmosphere at the present time. The introduction through recent legislation of the Council for the Accreditation of Teacher Education (CATE) has shown a will on the part of central government to take a more controlling part in the process. Much of the evidence so far has been that such interventions have been based upon misguided and ill-informed notions of what goes on within the training agencies. This book (having taken as its starting point the reflection of successful teachers upon their own training) provides hard evidence with which to challenge some of the more naïve ideas that are currently being promoted by politicians and even, at times, senior administrators in teacher training institutions. With the uncompromising stance, represented by its title, of establishing the centrality of the subject area within the teacher education process, the present volume never loses sight of the classroom, or of the school pupils, with which teacher education needs constantly to be concerned.

In the year this book is published, Robert Protherough retires from having been a teacher educator of great distinction in at least two very different institutions, in both of which I have had the privilege of working with him. It is fitting that his official career should conclude with his working with his co-author on a book that sums up the work that has concerned most of his working life. As his friend, as well as his editor, I would like to take the opportunity of thanking him for his contribution to English teaching and to wish him a productive, as well as a happy, retirement.

Anthony Adams

Introduction: the making of English teachers

This book is about a group of very different people who are alike in two respects: in their choice of a subject and in their choice of a profession. They are, in different ways and in different institutions, all teachers of English.

What does it actually mean, to be an English teacher; what does such a person know and do? What qualifies one for such a role? How do English teachers come to be? How far are they 'made' and what forces help to shape them? Does the notion of teaching English appeal to certain sorts of people, or does the job itself affect the sort of people they become? How do they actually view the nature of their ill-defined subject and the work they do in it? What gives them a sense of identity? Do they see themselves as different from teachers of other subjects? What sort of life-cycle do they have? What does it mean to 'get on', to have a successful career as an English teacher? Such apparently straightforward questions have rarely been answered, and we can detect three main reasons why this should be so.

The first reason is that perceptions of English as a subject (and thus of those who teach it) are so confused and so profoundly ambiguous, as will be indicated in our first chapter.[1] On the one hand English is seen to be at the heart of the curriculum, influencing learning in all subjects, taught more extensively to more pupils than anything else. There are more teachers with qualifications in English than in any other subject; until now English has occupied a greater proportion of the timetable in secondary schools than any other subject; more pupils are entered for 16+ examinations in English than for anything else. Children and parents alike see the subject as crucial. It is thought to offer essential preparation for adult life: necessary abilities for living in society and 'vocational skills' especially for the growing proportion of the population in professional, managerial, clerical and service work. In addition, voices still maintain that English must somehow be charged with preserving human values in a technological society.

On the other hand, however, English is seen as having no real separate identity, as being soft and easy, without any obvious vocational application, a subject that everyone 'knows'. Partly because the skills of the subject are seen as so important and partly because everyone feels competent to have an opinion on it, any supposed failure on the part of English teachers is greeted with indignation and hostility. No other group is so frequently attacked in the media, and during the writing of this book supposed weaknesses in grammar, in reading and in spelling were each the subject of bitter criticism. There are repeated cries, often in the face of the evidence, that 'standards' are falling, allegations that English teachers are somehow subversive, and there is a desire to impose a curriculum and methodology that will 'bring them into line'. From the very beginning there has been conflict and disagreement about what should actually go on in classrooms under the name of English, and about what goals the subject should be trying to achieve. Control of English is seen as one means of establishing ideological control over society and many pressure groups long to exert that influence.

The second reason is that the uninformed prejudice and heady emotion that have always dominated discussions of English, as suggested above, have had little to do with facts about the men and women who actually teach it. There has been no serious enquiry in this country into how English teachers come to be or into their subsequent careers; little examination of their views or of the ways in which perceptions of the subject are related to practice in the classroom. This country has seen nothing like the massive enquiry into the training and development of English teachers in the United States, published as early as 1961, or the wide-ranging Australian conference which led to a book called *English in Teacher Education*.[2] There has been no real attempt to consider the recruitment of English teachers, their qualifications and the nature of their preparation, the heavy use of non-specialists, the conditions under which teaching has to go on, the new demands that are being made (and the lack of resources for these) or the restricted opportunities for continuing development. The focus of this book is on that strange omission.

The third reason concerns the parallel mixture of ignorance and prejudice in thinking about ways in which English teachers should be prepared for their work. Years of indifference have been succeeded by a frenetic attempt to pin all the blame for unsatisfactory schooling on those who conduct professional education programmes. The ill-informed attacks (and equally ill-informed blanket solutions) thrive on the dearth of research into teacher education. As Professor William Taylor has said, 'Too little time and effort has been devoted to the systematic study of how teachers are educated and trained'.[3] Tony Becher's excellent recent study of the academic community points out under the heading 'unfinished business' the need for research into the 'relatively neglected' but important applied academic fields like education, and the urgent need to relate academic specialisms to their existence as school subjects.[4] Brian Doyle has pointed out that even the best discussions of the evolution of English studies fail to relate the cultural and political changes to 'the consciousness of professional teachers'.[5] At this level, the 'meager [sic] amount of literature on English teacher preparation'[6] reflects the reality beneath the rhetoric: a lack of real concern for the subject and the perceptions of those actually involved in it. Shortages of mathematics or physics teachers regularly make the headlines; the equal (possibly greater) shortages of English teachers are ignored. There have been many studies of those who specialize in teaching the sciences or languages, but only recently has there appeared any serious analysis of those who study English.[7] This volume grows to some extent from that, and the two should be seen as complementary. The perceptions of students and those of staff can be separated for convenience, but they are inevitably bound up together.

This volume attempts to provide some of the material for a more reasoned discussion about the ways in which English teachers are shaped and shape themselves, although inevitably it also mirrors the convictions of its authors. It places the current state of affairs, what is, in the context of what has been and of what might be. It assumes that the quality of any educational system depends on the quality of its teachers. The concept of a special person to teach English is a relatively recent one, and throughout the subsequent period there has been continual disagreement about what such a person should be like or should do. Drawing on a series of detailed questionnaires and interviews, this book considers those who are recruited as English teachers, the nature of their initial professional education and the basis on which they are certified as proficient, their induction into the school system, their further professional study, updating and preparation for new roles, and their career structure. It relates available information on these topics to teachers' perceptions of them.

It is necessary to say from the start that the group of English teachers considered in detail here is not a scientifically balanced sample – if, indeed, such a thing were possible to achieve. Our aim was much more selective. We wanted to concentrate on a fairly small number who might reasonably be regarded by others as examples of 'good practice' (to quote a favourite phrase of Her Majesty's Inspectors). Our method was to write to a large number of English advisers in different parts of the country and to a small number of established English tutors in university Departments of Education, asking them to approach one or two teachers known to them whom they would rate as particularly effective English practitioners. In such stirring times as these, it is not surprising that some advisers felt under too much pressure to help us. Fortunately, however, we received enough assistance to enable us to locate just over the one hundred teachers that had been our target (110, to be precise). As will be seen in Chapter 2, it is an extremely varied group – in age, qualifications, experience and attitudes – except in the one common respect of perceived effectiveness in English teaching.

The following chapters consider how notions of what English teachers are and might be have come to be formulated. We discuss their backgrounds, qualifications and careers, drawing largely on the experiences of our 110. We examine the kinds of initial preparation that have been offered to those intending to become English teachers, and look at other possible ways in which this work might be carried out. Four experienced teacher-educators describe the very different courses in which they are involved and reflect on the current situation. We consider the development and changes that English teachers experience during their careers as they make and re-make themselves. Finally, we present a personal, perhaps idealistic, view of how things might be better. At a time of acrimonious debate, we are well aware of the wide range of responses that different individuals will make to our diagnosis and our prescriptions. Nevertheless, our hope is that English teachers, teacher-educators, policy-makers and others will all find something that can be helpfully applied to their own situations, because the current argument about the making of English teachers is a crucial one, and all members of the profession need to be involved in it.

1　Shaping the image of an English teacher

The pre-history of English teaching

Before we can begin to discuss the making of English teachers, we have to consider to whom that term applies. For how long has there been a separate, identifiable group that could be called English teachers? Not very long, certainly. Before the turn of the century, there was no subject 'English' (in the sense of an acknowledged, unified field of study) for them to teach.[1] The regulations of the 1890s treated 'English' as concerned solely with parsing and analysis, quite separate from reading, composition and literature, which might all be in the hands of different teachers.[2] Years later in London's elementary schools what we should consider English was still being divided and timetabled as nine separate 'subjects'.[3] Even while the subject was gaining wider acceptance in the early years of this century (made compulsory in State schools by the 1904 Regulations; its 'claim to a definite place in the curriculum of every secondary school' asserted by the Board of Education report of 1910) it is clear that the various English activities were not seen as the responsibility of one teacher. Indeed, that Report had to argue strongly that literature and composition were not *really* separate subjects, and that it was 'eminently desirable' that the same teacher should be responsible for both.[4]

A decade later, the Historical Retrospect of the Newbolt Report opens by remarking that the subject has 'scarcely any history': 'Of conscious and direct teaching of English the past affords little sign'.[5] In the public and grammar schools, 'English was not seriously considered as an educational subject' (para. 105) and further up the educational hierarchy, 'it is not too much to say that, till quite lately, English had no position at all in the Universities' (191) and 'the serious study of English Language and Literature is a comparatively new one' (193).

To discuss what English teachers do, are, and might be, it is essential to be aware of the framing historical processes by which they have come to be. Looking back, we can detect three overlapping phases resulting from universal compulsory education and the development of an increasingly specialized curriculum at secondary level. A concern for the discrete skills of English was slowly followed by the gradual establishing of English as a separate subject in the curriculum, and later still by the appointment of English teachers specifically responsible for it. As one significant study concluded, before the twentieth century 'there were certainly very few teachers who could be called or would have called themselves teachers of English'.[6]

Even for the next twenty years, circumstances were such that very few would have chosen to describe themselves in such a way. 'English' activities had a low social status because over the centuries the teaching of functional literacy to the working class had been seen as unskilled labour, and the reading of English literature was only for girls (while their brothers studied the classics). More profoundly, though, who could have been given the title of English teacher? Teachers in elementary schools would not have thought of themselves in such a way, for they were to work as generalists across the whole curriculum. (In the same way today, although some primary teachers will have specialized in English and may have responsibility for curriculum leadership in that subject, few refer to themselves as English teachers.) The certificated teachers, who in any case made up less than a third of those in elementary schools,[7] were trained in English grammar, reading, recitation, handwriting and English literature among the many other subjects to be 'covered' and examined, but there is no suggestion either of English as a single field of study or of teachers being specially trained for it. As late as 1929, English was just one of ten subjects to be included in training and when subject specialism did begin to appear, it was in other areas like physical education, music, art, woodwork and metalwork.[8]

At secondary level also, when the training of teachers began to expand after the 1902 Act, English was seen as a necessary qualification for entrants, but not as a subject for specialist training. Because the university degree was thought an adequate preparation, and training was regarded as socially demeaning, the absence of degree courses in English ensured both the low status of that subject in schools and the lack of qualified teachers to teach it. Such an inevitable correlation between English Literature as a university subject and the training of teachers had been pointed out in the 1880s. Arguing for the establishment of the subject at Oxford as a way of disseminating it more widely, John Churton Collins wrote that its ability to fulfil that function 'depends obviously on the training of its teachers, and the training of its teachers depends as obviously on the willingness or the unwillingness of the Universities to provide that training'.[9]

Because of the relative unwillingness of the universities to contemplate either English or education as academic subjects,[10] it was not until the 1920s and later that graduate English teachers began to emerge in any numbers, and the subject was not regarded as a desirable or even necessary specialism in the public and grammar schools to which most graduates went. According to one headmaster, in 1918 English was viewed with 'belittlement', 'distrust' and 'contempt'.[11] The same author (lamenting the 'few and fumbling' attempts of classics teachers to work with English literature) anticipated a future in which English graduates might take their place in schools, developing new methods, linking reading with writing 'as the importance of their subject becomes more and more recognised'.[12] But that still lay ahead.

A different indication of the late emergence of English teachers can be found in imaginative writing. One major study of the way in which teachers are depicted in literature[13] has discovered that although portraits of classicists, scientists and modern language teachers, among others, are common from the late nineteenth century onwards, English teachers do not appear as such before about 1930. Some English *teaching*, mostly by classicists, does go on as a minor subject in books like Roger Wray's *The Soul of a Teacher* (1915) or S.P.B. Mais's *A Schoolmaster's Diary* (1918) but – despite the campaigning zeal of Mais – it is clear that secondary English was essentially in the hands of non-specialists. Mr Kenneth, the 'English master' in Henry Williamson's *Dandelion Days* (1930) is a teacher of English *subjects*, that also include history and geography. In the same year, however, Alaric Jacob's novel *Seventeen* introduced a young master, Mr Dilke, specifically as an English teacher, with a number of marked characteristics. He wears plus-fours and decorates his room with black lacquer furniture; he has 'advanced' literary and artistic tastes and does not play games; he founds a literary society and causes a furore by studying the works of D.H. Lawrence. The author wrote:

> That he made a sensation would be to put it mildly. He was the sole topic of conversation for twenty-four hours, at the end of which time his clothes, manners, speech and past history had been so pulled to pieces that of the poor man's charac- ter there remained only the bare bones ... a dude, a dago and a dandy ... an outsider ... a wild and woolly Bohemian.[14]

Innovations are usually mocked, as we can see from the pages of *Punch*. This novel suggests that at the beginning of the 1930s the idea of an English master in a boarding school was still a novelty to be caricatured. A new stereotype – the English teacher as progressive, controversial, different – was in the making. What that has come to mean will be seen from the views expressed later in this chapter, in the section 'What sort of animal is an English teacher?'

The significance of the Newbolt Report

We owe the modern concept of an English teacher, symbolically at least, to the publication of the Newbolt Report, *The Teaching of English in England*, in 1921. By defining English in a quite new way, it created a climate in which English teaching as a specialized profession became inevitable. One simple way of suggesting its influence is to examine the number of texts published on English teaching at different periods. Whereas very few volumes with *Teaching of English* in their titles appeared in the first twenty years of this century, at least thirteen significant books so named were issued between 1921 and 1932.

In the Report, 'English' was no longer used to describe a conglomerate of separate skills or a group of 'English subjects', but as a single, organic, all-embracing term for a unique, central school subject, requiring – by impli-cation – special men and women to teach it. The particular concepts that animated the Committee were by no means new,[15] but the novelty lay in bring-ing together under the title of English, 'taught as a fine art', four separate concepts: the universal need for literacy as the core of the curriculum, the de-velopmental importance of children's self-expression, a belief in the power of English literature for moral and social improvement, and a concern for 'the full development of mind and character'. The frontiers of the subject were thus pushed out to cover a whole range of mental, emotional, imaginative, moral and spiritual goals: 'almost convertible with thought', 'a method' as well as 'a subject' that 'must have entry everywhere' (para. 57).

This largely expedient and perhaps deliberately ambiguous map of the subject, colonizing areas that had previously lain within other disciplines, has been enormously influential. After the sufferings and doubts of the 1914–18 war, English as a newly-minted subject was invested with the resonance of 'Englishness', defined through the English language and supremely through the heritage of English literature. It was through a shared experience of English, said the Report, drawing on Matthew Arnold, that the social class divisions of the country could be healed and a 'national culture' be established.[16] The committee could hardly have foreseen that a series of debates and divisions lasting into the 1990s would centre on these inter-connected definitions of English culture, of the literary heritage and of the teaching and learning of English. Henry Widdowson could justifiably complain in his note of reservation to the Kingman Report that 'what English is on the curriculum *for*, is not really explored here with any rigour'.[17]

The Newbolt Report is thin on practical details about the kinds of teaching that might achieve its aims, or about the kinds of English teacher that might be needed. In proposing a quite new curricular framework, the Committee had no existing tradition to draw on. A new sort of subject would demand new kinds of teachers to remedy the failings of the past and present and to bring about the aspirations for the future. The section headings repeatedly use words like neglect, problem, lack, difficulties, and misapprehensions. English *should* be 'the only basis possible for a national education' (para. 9), 'the one indispensable preliminary and foundation of all the rest' which must 'take precedence of all other branches of learning' (6), 'the essential basis of a liberal education for all English people' (13). By contrast with this ideal, however, the members of the Committee said that what they found in actuality was 'an altogether inadequate recognition of the place of English in an Englishman's education' (para. 191, echoing 1), caused by a failure to establish the subject as important in schools and universities and by the parallel failure to attract and train teachers for it.

The laudable ambitions for English as a subject depended – as the Committee realized – on the provision of appropriately qualified teachers, but the Report reveals a basic uncertainty about what those appropriate qualifications are, and indeed about what good English teaching might actually look like. (The next section considers the ambiguity about whether English teachers should be specialists.) The Report admits that 'the methods of teaching English have yet to be explored' (para. 101), and adds that at secondary level, 'probably the greatest obstacle to improvement hitherto has been the absence of a good tradition in the teaching of English' (109). It quotes an Inspectors' Memorandum on the 'unfortunate' truth that 'methods of teaching English are so far little developed. They have been far less thought out than the methods of teaching some other subjects' (117). Three years later, making the best of a bad job and referring vaguely to 'the many difficult questions of method involved in the teaching of English', the Board of Education remarked hopefully that at least 'in developing his [sic] method the teacher of English has the advantage of being bound by no tradition'.[18]

Looking back, with the benefit of hindsight, it is possible to see how several distinct but powerful strands of thinking came together in the 1920s to create a model of English teaching that was formative. In bold over-simplification we can detect three of these. First there was the missionary role of English, called on to confront the forces of industrialism and to counter the growing influence of the media. The recurrent images in the Report were of people being starved while weeds flourished in the fields; of the power of literature to feed, to purify, to unify, to redeem. Margaret Mathieson has argued that in a time of crisis the functions traditionally attributed to religious faith were attached to a new and idealistic view of English teaching.[19] This idea ran through the Newbolt Report, and was given celebrated expression in George Sampson's claim that the purpose of education is 'not to prepare children for their occupations, but to prepare children against their occupations'.[20] Second, there was the Dewey-inspired emphasis on learning by doing, the notion that English should develop creativity, foreshadowed in the 1910 recommendations about the importance of oral work and by the influence of men like Caldwell Cook.[21] Third, in an age when the influence of the classics was waning, English was seen as the chief way of conveying a cultural tradition, developing sensitivity and moral awareness. For most children, literature would mean English literature. Such a view was pushed to its logical conclusion by F.R. Leavis, who in 1930 argued that teachers of English were ultimately responsible for the health of the language, for the growth of moral values and eventually for the whole quality of life itself.[22] At Cambridge in particular the 'missionary' emphasis of the Newbolt Report was re-framed with specific attention to what should be taught and how. This, as Francis Mulhern has argued, emphasized the notion of a professional career in English centering on talent rather than on establishment values of birth and breeding.[23] By contrast with an academic English hierarchy that had become inward-looking in its obsession with establishing professional status, the *Scrutiny* group looked out to society, and particularly to the wider education system.

These three trends combined to give a seductively important role to English teachers. They were called to be the élite of the profession, concerned not simply with teaching a subject, but with the total personal and social development of pupils and with the health of society. By 1930 English was becoming a dominant university discipline. 'In terms of its eventually achieved overall influence, at both institutional and symbolic levels, the success of English proved to be more dramatic than that of any other subject'.[24] It is hardly surprising, then, that many of its graduates were turning to teaching. It seemed that no work could be more serious or more rewarding.

Should English teachers be specialists?

The Newbolt Committee, echoing the Board of Education report of eleven years earlier, was anxious to refute the common belief that 'any master or mistress can teach English' and to assert the need for 'definite qualifications', but still had to temporize about what those qualifications might be: 'They need not indeed be specialists in the strict sense of the word ...' (para. 7). That significant concession recurs throughout the work of the Committee. In part this was because of the celebrated insistence, often echoed since, that 'every teacher is a teacher of English, because every teacher is a teacher in English' (64), which less helpfully implied that the role of English teaching can be subsumed across the curriculum. In part it arose from a realistic recognition that there was no immediate likelihood of changing the situation in which nearly all English was being taught by people who had no specific training, qualifications (or in some cases interest) in the subject: 'a suitable matter to be entrusted to any member of the staff who had some free time at his [sic] disposal' (6).

George Sampson also wrote of the convenient assumption that no special expertise was required to teach English: 'I suppose there isn't an elementary school teacher in the country who does not feel perfectly capable of teaching all the English needed in elementary schools. I wonder how many there really are'.[25] According to an estimate quoted in the Newbolt Report, 'certainly not more than one-third' of those leaving college with a certificate were 'qualified to take English with a class' (para. 165).

While arguing against the scornful notion that English teaching is 'a task which any teacher can perform' (para. 117), the Newbolt Report admits that some specialists in other subjects are also effective English teachers, that 'much good work in English literature can be done by teachers who have not been trained as specialists', although it goes on to specify that they should have 'good knowledge, interest, and the gift of communicating their own enthusiasm' (130). What sort of knowledge and interest? There is a pervasive vagueness about necessary qualifications. The Report says that for English 'no teacher can, in his [sic] own grade, be too highly gifted or too highly trained' (17). What sort of gifts, and what sorts of training? The question is posed – 'it may be asked how far it is desirable to entrust it to a specialist teacher' (82) – but is never answered; the need for better teaching is accompanied by the remark 'whether or not a scheme of specialisation is adopted'.

This desire that English should be taught by special kinds of people, combined with a reluctance to claim that they should have undergone a special kind of education in English, accounts for the fuzziness that marks much of the sections on teachers: 'we have no wish to prescribe any one kind of preliminary training as essential' (para. 129). The committee had still not really thrown off the view that any one of the right kind (whatever that might be) could teach English. The crucial passage is this:

> The English teacher who has studied other subjects at the University – whether Classics, modern languages, history, or philosophy – has gained in breadth and in power by so doing; so has the teacher who has studied music, painting, architecture, or some branch of natural science. On the other hand, the teacher who has specialised in English at the University ought to have an advantage in scientific thoroughness and grasp of his [sic] subject. (129)

The ultimate balance seems in favour of the non-specialist, who *has* gained in power and breadth, rather than the English student who 'ought' to have a more thorough grasp. We must remember, of course, that the Committee itself was largely composed of academics who had read subjects other than English.

It is perhaps not surprising, then, that when describing as 'a matter of great moment' the provision of 'an adequate teaching staff' (para. 16), the Report skirts delicately around the question of whether or not English should ideally be in the hands of specialists. It simply proposes that all teachers should be equipped to instruct in English language, and that literature should be in the hands of someone who has 'received an education of the kind towards which he [sic] is to lead his class'. That 'kind' would probably have been gained through the study of the classics or modern languages. Later in the Report it is claimed that it was in classics that 'the large majority of the best teachers of English Literature to-day received their University training' (197).

George Sampson pointed out that this conclusion was hardly surprising, since classical masters were the only ones who had received an education in language and literature.[26] He was much more robust in refuting the notion that 'the traditional classical curriculum gave a general mental alertness and strength that was valid for all purposes of life'.[27] Like Nowell Smith a year or two earlier, he found little sign that the intense study of the classics by the privileged few had been of lasting benefit: 'one cannot help being amazed at the low standard of literary culture in the rank and file of the classes from which this *élite* has been drawn'.[28] He admitted the point made in the Newbolt Report, but questioned its application: 'Many excellent masters can teach, and do teach, good English through Latin or Greek or French or German; but that is because they are excellent teachers, not because they teach foreign languages'. His conclusion was the strongest affirmation up to that time of the need for English specialists: 'This affectation of making every other accomplishment in English depend upon some other language is an evil tradition'; 'English must be learnt from English'.[29]

The uncertainty of the Newbolt Committee was maintained in a Board of

Education report three years later, which still placed the notion of a 'specialist' English teacher in quotes and referred to 'the English teacher, specifically so styled' as though this were an unfamiliar concept.[30] That report also saw it as 'neither necessary, nor desirable' that all English teachers should have been trained in the subject: Others 'may have built their special knowledge on a basis of history ... the classics ... the language and literature of France, or Italy, or Germany' (para. 42). The furthest the Report goes is to suggest that 'whenever a school has such a specialist' he [sic] should be accorded the same status as a senior teacher of mathematics or modern languages (129).

For many years, indeed, the impression remained in public and grammar schools that English was actually better in the hands of teachers who had specialized in other subjects. Lord James has told us that, as late as 1945, when he went to Manchester Grammar School, only one member of that very large staff was qualified in English.[31] It is hard to throw off the legacy of the past. For whatever motives of principle or expediency, the fact remains that something like a fifth of all secondary English teaching has remained in the hands of people with no qualification whatsoever in the subject beyond experience.[32]

What sort of animal is an English teacher?

The emergence of English as a coherent subject demanded the creation of a quite new kind of teacher, shaped in ways that had not previously been considered. The recommendations of the Newbolt Report implied that such a person would require a literary training (though hardly of the kind then offered by English degree courses), a range of personal qualities (sensitivity, understanding), an ability to unlock the creative potential of children (then the province of educational psychology), a social concern for all kinds of children, and some (largely undefined) expertise in language. English teachers were not to be concerned with vocational or utilitarian training ('commercial English is objectionable' because 'the needs of business are best met by a liberal education' – recommendation 30). Nor was their chief concern the imparting of knowledge, but the changing of lives. This depended on establishing a special relationship between teacher and taught ('there is no lesson like the poetry lesson for producing that intimacy between teacher and class which makes school a happy place' – para. 92).

In this crucial respect George Sampson was at one with the official report: both were clear that English was unlike many other school subjects, in that it required essential personal qualities that could not be guaranteed by formal academic qualifications. Sampson said that the English teacher's chief concern was 'not the minds he [sic] can measure but the souls he can save'.[33] This concern for personal qualities was to become a recurrent note from 1921 onwards. Quotations above have indicated the Committee's desire to ground an

English teacher's abilities in 'necessary insight and enthusiasm' (para. 11), 'knowledge, interest, and the gift of communicating their own enthusiasm' (130), rather than in any particular specialism. Indeed they quote the celebrated (or notorious) judgement that 'the ideal teacher is born, not made' (129). Sampson made the comparison with other subjects specific: 'University qualifications are a safe enough guide when you are looking for acquirements – when you want a science master or a history master; but not when you are choosing someone to be a medium for the transmission of the spirit'.[34] In his conclusion he laments that: 'We have never insisted that the chief and crowning qualification of an English teacher is ability to teach English' – an early expression of the idea that peda- gogic not academic qualities are of most importance. (He does, of course, agree that the two may coexist; they are not alternatives.) His view, which must have seemed insanely idealistic at the time, has turned out to be true and prophetic. The only reason that the right sort of English teachers did not exist, he writes, is that society had never asked for them. 'Let the paramount claim of English be admitted and teachers will shape themselves and be shaped for the task of teach- ing it'.

The lasting influence of these ideas is seen in the responses of our one hundred 'effective' teachers. When asked if they felt that English teachers were somehow different from those working in other subjects, only six felt that there was little or no difference (and four of these six are now working as advisers). Their minority view was that English teachers *see* themselves as different, but that 'there is little evidence for this'; 'a lot of this is in the eye of the beholder'. An English teacher turned deputy head commented that 'some of them are very interested in the ways in which they think they are different ...'.

That interest revealed itself in the responses of the great majority who did believe that a difference existed. Occasionally this was described at a surface level ('longer hair, more earrings' or 'more English teachers smoke'), but when asked how they would define the difference, 36 per cent pointed to particular personal qualities, 28 per cent to personal attitudes and 37 per cent to different relationships with pupils. On the positive side, they would like to consider themselves as people who are 'nicer', 'more open, more imaginative, more inter-active', 'more concerned with humanity', 'passionate about their subject', 'more tolerant, less moralistic', 'possessed of dry, ironic wit', 'more energetic (and they need to be)', even 'better educated than many'. On the other hand, many of the comments quoted above are linked by their authors to more critical balancing perceptions: 'often hopelessly impractical', 'more vain and arrogant', simultaneously 'cleverer, stroppier, saintlier, more put upon'. One remarked that 'poor English teachers are worse than those of other subjects'. A number believed that English teachers are 'more politically aware', 'much more progress- ive', 'mavericks', 'likely to be subversive', though one commented that if 'we tend to be more generally perceived as subversive' then 'the revolution will wait a long time if it depends on our anarchies!'

Typical comments about 'good relations with students', 'better relationships with children', suggested in very broad terms that English teachers were 'more sensitive to pupil needs', 'more aware of the centrality of the pupil', 'more understanding of young people's sense of *their* world', 'more in touch with learners', showing 'a wish to connect with young people's experiences'. This meant in school that 'they tend to be more aware of process in learning'; they are more conscious of 'collaborative learning, of the nature of learning, of the importance of affective and aesthetic development'; 'their response to children's work requires more flexibility/insight/penetration/work/time ...'.

Half of the sample felt that English teachers worked in the classroom in a different way from teachers of other subjects, and one in five referred to particular kinds of teacher behaviour that they thought distinguished English staff. For some this simply consisted in the fact that 'they work harder'! As one remarked sardonically, 'an Art teacher does not carry home with her/him thirty pictures to mark'. Others were more specific about the constraints and opportunities: 'English teachers tend to do whatever they like!' because 'there is no fixed syllabus for each year'; 'they do not go on teaching the same syllabus with minor variations'; 'they can never relax into feeling that they've covered the syllabus'. There were indications of a continuing need to teach against the system. One said that 'because the basis of their work is (or should be) human growth and development, they will always be frustrated by the demands of a system designed to inject children with knowledge'. Another commented that 'they tend to be more aware of cultural activities and their importance to survival in a disgusting world'.

English teachers are 'prepared to take risks', they are 'more willing to seek new strategies/methods/ideas to implement in their teaching', 'they depend less on bought resources, more on spinning things out of their own imagination', 'they ask their pupils to challenge accepted views rather than learn them'. As 'custodians of what appears to be the most popular subject in the majority of schools', they are challenged by the need to be 'so omniscient.... Parents demand a high standard from us because of the importance placed on the subject ... you are very accountable'.

There is little point in asking whether these judgements are 'true'. Such views from the classroom are important, however, as an indication of how English teachers see themselves and their subject today, an odd mixture of the clear-eyed and the idealistic. The overall impression echoes that of the authorities analysed by Margaret Mathieson, who concluded that the different views 'all turned, finally, to the teacher's personality as being the crucial element in English in schools'.[35] This does not mean, of course, that they all wanted the same sort of personality – indeed they pointed to quite dissimilar qualities – but the heavy emphasis on personality and on relationships does seem to mark off English teachers from others. The demands of this subject stress 'how very good, as a person, the good English teacher needs to be', because from the beginning 'specially high optimism has been invested in English as the subject most likely to achieve desirable results'.[36] The first significant official report on the subject in

1910, rejecting any notion of an agreed or imposed syllabus, formulated the difference in these terms: 'English is the last subject in which a teacher should be bound by hard and fast rules. No subject gives more scope for individuality of treatment or for varied experiment; in none is the personal quality of the teacher more important'.[37] This stress on the individual and personal has remained significant in all subsequent discussions. Whereas other subjects are seen by pupils as either enjoyable or important, English alone is seen as both.[38]

To be a special kind of person, to teach a subject that in many ways is more than a subject and that has major repercussions outside the classroom walls, has imposed a special responsibility on English teachers, and helps to explain why they are so vulnerable to criticism. Administrators are more comfortable with subjects that have clearly defined specialist knowledge with firm academic boundaries and that are remote from what is learned within the home and the community. A head of department told us of an occasion when she was seeking an additional member of staff. The Head produced a recent advertisement, and suggested that this would do, with another word substituted for 'historian'. 'What word do you use for someone who teaches English?' he asked, and was not satisfied with the answer, 'English teacher'. Proper subjects are taught by people called historians, geographers, physicists and modern linguists, he implied; knowledge of the subject rather than the teaching of it is primary. By contrast, new definitions of English, new ranking of objectives, new styles of teaching, take on additional significance that is not limited to the subject classroom, because 'changing English is changing schooling'[39] – and potentially even more than that. What James Donald has called 'the intractable problem' of English teaching is that 'it remains trapped within its sense of being called to a social and cultural mission – whether healing the State or empowering people to escape its oppressions'.[40] Arguments about what should, or should not, be read in school, about 'correctness' in talk or writing, about assessment and so on, are actually arguments about shaping young people's views of the world. Reflecting on his Working Group's report, Professor Brian Cox has said that 'a National Curriculum in English is intimately involved with questions about our national identity, indeed with the whole future ethos of British society. The teaching of English ... affects the individual and social identity of us all'.[41]

English has a special power to challenge conventions, institutions, governments, business interests – any established system. This resides in the fact that English is concerned with the uncontrollable power of a shared language that we all speak and the uncontrollable responses to what we read. The work of English teaching involves continual pressing for the expression of alternative ideas, inviting challenge to received opinions, seeking strong personal responses, establishing debate. The teacher's special relationship with students depends on democratic openness, not on knowing the answers. The subject matter of English lessons is likely to draw on the actual interests and experiences of pupils, where they may be more informed than those who teach them. It is often said that English teachers are more in tune with youth culture than those who work in other subjects. At times their students may be permitted to voice rebellious or revolutionary ideas, or they may do so without permission.

One result of this is that English teachers are often perceived in the staff-room and beyond, as being 'progressive' or anti-authoritarian. From the 1960s onwards, English teachers seemed to be at the forefront of movements for change in organization, teaching and assessment. Consequently they have served as convenient scapegoats for Right-wing politicians and the popular press, anxious to pin on them responsibility for supposedly falling standards of literacy, for hooliganism, and for virtually any social and economic problems. According to Margaret Mathieson, 'progressive English teachers are likely to experience strains and tensions that are more severe than those felt by other members of staff',[42] because their aims and roles are less secure, and because they are less likely to feel at one with other staff, with parents and with society. They are more likely to be involved in conflicts over 'unsuitable' texts, 'improper' language, 'undesirable' topics and 'unprofessional' attitudes. Radical approaches tend to be associated with radical politics. The shift away from prescriptive English teaching involved a major shift in the relationship between teacher and taught. Over forty years ago, Raymond O'Malley remarked that English teachers have to help their students 'to face successfully every challenge and invitation of the life around them'.[43] Such teachers are likely to receive confidences and intimate revelations that can be hard to handle and that may lead to confrontations with authority, 'management', colleagues or parents. 'The somewhat disturbing implication for English teachers seems to be that hostile reactions to their work indicate the extent to which they are being successful'.[44]

What does an English teacher teach?

The last section commented on the almost universal view that English teachers are somehow different from those that teach other subjects. This subjective belief is grounded in a more objective understanding of the uniqueness of their subject. All major studies comment on this. One recent book, from the first page onwards, repeatedly uses words like 'unique', 'distinctive', and 'special' to describe English studies.[45] In curricular terms, it is easy to list reasons why this should be so: the subject is uniquely poised between school and the wider life. Only a small part of the teaching of English is carried out by English teachers; children arrive at school with a wealth of existing language experience; the goals of English are not simply subject-specific ones, but are concerned with all aspects of learning and living. English teaches the abilities that underlie the learning of all other subjects. English lessons are concerned with all aspects of the individual; thoughts and feelings are inseparable; students' responses are an essential element of what is being studied; individual differences are often more significant than universal truths. Because there is no generally agreed body of subject matter, the boundaries of the subject are notoriously unclear and cannot be neatly defined.

It is significant that during the upheavals of the 1980s there has been such a flood of books posing basic theoretical questions about what English is or should be. Simply to consider the many titles is enough, with their emphasis on re-reading, re-writing or re-ordering the tradition, on changes, new directions or perspectives, on widening, extending or even exploding the subject.[46] People have talked so much of the 'crisis' in English studies that the prophecy has become self-fulfilling. As different models (or paradigms) of English teaching have successively come under attack, it has become plain both that there is no return to some 'innocent' English and also that there is little prospect of replacing English with some agreed alternative, whatever it might be called (Cultural Studies or Textual Studies, according to some). As Francis Mulhern has argued, 'we face a situation in which a maximum of intellectual attack, a maximum of desire to reconstruct the subject, coincide with a near-minimum of institutional opportunity'.[47]

It is hardly surprising, then, that the younger teachers in our survey expressed uncertainty about the nature of their subject: 'English has emerged as a much wider subject than I had anticipated'. Even the most experienced are still tentative, saying 'there are no certainties' or 'I think it is more complex now than I thought (and I thought it "the hardest subject to teach" then)'. Examining the terminology, the underlying images, used by our sample of English teachers helps to define their sense of subject identity, to establish the hidden curriculum which affects the way in which they make sense of the world, or initiate students and new teachers into the community. Their comments illustrate the validity of the Cox Report's judgement about different, co-existing models of the subject:

> It is possible to identify within the English teaching profession a number of different views of the subject.... We stress that they are not the only possible views, they are not sharply distinguishable, and they are certainly not mutually exclusive.... Teachers of English will differ in the weight they give to each of these views of the subject.[48]

Many teachers offered views of the subject that fit neatly enough into one or another of the five generalized models put forward in the Report.

1 *A personal growth view*. 'The basis of our work is (or should be) human growth and development'; 'nurturing individual development'; 'aware of the centrality of the pupil'; 'our "subject" is so close to the learner – *is* the learner and the process of learning'; 'growth of the whole person through expressive explorations'.

2 *A cross-curricular view*. 'I see it now as being part of the whole curriculum, and see much more how things should link'; 'English will have to become less introverted and accept the cross-curricular development'; 'language is central to all learning so English teachers have a great responsibility'; 'they bear a significant responsibility for the development of language skills and thus help to determine how "accessible" the school curriculum is for pupils in all areas'.

3 *An adult needs view*. 'I see English more as a tool to develop social skills and

preparation for the world of work'; 'our subject is a service subject'; 'more need to justify its value in a vocation-orientated curriculum'; 'inner resources and an external structure to deal with the world outside school'.

4 *A cultural heritage view.* 'It consists in maximum exposure to literature'; 'saving literature from being marginalised'; 'I believed in bringing great literature to children'; 'As a product of *Use of English* teachers and taught by Leavis sympathisers at university, I went into teaching with those assumptions'.

5 *A cultural analysis view.* 'I've realised its situation within cultural and political frameworks'; 'I see English ... in terms of developing autonomy and critical awareness – skills and attitudes'; 'cultural development model'; 'a need to assimilate the conceptual revolution of post-structuralist thought'; 'root English in a social view of language'; 'need to reflect multi-racial society'.

Possibly more striking are the comments which implicitly establish a comparison between different models, rejecting some or claiming to have abandoned one in favour of another. Teachers write, for example, of resisting the pressures to cater for the 'needs of technology and form-filling' or 'the further rise of instrumental rationality via TVEI, etc.'; they say that English 'must not be seen as a service medium' or talk of their 'refusal to see the subject English simply as a garage servicing the needs and demands of other subject areas'; they fear that 'the experience of literature of many children will be diminished' or defend 'cultural activities and their importance to survival'. In a number of cases they reveal a change of perception ('I now see ...') and of practice, a paradigm shift. 'I no longer have a passionate commitment to Great Literature', says one; another now sees pupils as 'human beings in complex social interactions rather than spirits to be nurtured'; a third records that teaching is 'now less (a) literary (b) personal/affective, and more sociologically, politically informed'; a fourth says 'originally I placed too much emphasis on "lit." (having come through school then university) instead of language skills'. More is said about this awareness of change in Chapter 9 of this volume.

Such a range of views and such evidence of re-thinking bear witness to two points raised in the Cox Report: the scale and uncertain boundaries of the subject ('such broadness poses problems' – 2.2) and the impossibility of establishing fixed, permanent principles ('views about English teaching have developed and changed over the past 20 years and will continue to do so' – 2.4). One study has examined the ways in which 'beginning teachers are entering PGCE English programmes having undergone a radically different kind of English undergraduate degree from that experienced by their future colleagues who graduated some years before them'.[49] Within schools, the teachers who responded were conscious of doing so in a period of unprecedented change in curriculum, assessment, theory and administration. A number of them were uneasily aware of sharp divisions within their English departments. They referred to the problems for a new teacher on joining a group of colleagues where there is no consensus about principles and practices. It is very hard to know whether or not one is being successful, particularly if colleagues judge by quite different criteria. In such circumstances it is hardly surprising that post-graduate courses in English education often begin (like the one at Oxford described later in this volume or the one at Hull) by emphasizing the diversity of views rather than any consensus, or go on (like the course at Stirling, also described in a later chapter) to analyse 'the strengths and weaknesses' of 'different modes of teaching', rather than making any pretence of selecting one 'best buy'.

When they were asked, 'What do you see as the most urgent problems facing English teachers at this time?', 30 per cent referred to problems concerning the definition or modelling of the subject itself. They mentioned, for example, 'confusion about what "English" is and does', 'maintaining and promoting the special "Englishness" of English', 'the need to reaffirm the type of model of English teaching just described', 'developing a coherent rationale for the subject', 'insecurity regarding the nature of English as a discipline', 'how to maintain an English identity', or – more specifically – 'to fight an over-simplified view of language study as the centre of English studies', 'to establish English among the Arts', 'maintenance of the "progressive" ideal' or 'thinking clearly about what would happen to pedagogy if we accepted the Eagleton camp-followers as gurus'. There is clearly no consensus here about what is to count as English.

The next chapter considers in some detail what these English teachers are like, their qualifications and how they come to be. It examines their perceptions of what a career in English teaching might involve and discusses the problems of 'making' English teachers who will match the needs of schools.

2 Making careers in English teaching

Successful English teachers

How can we describe the variety of skilled English teachers represented by our sample of over a hundred individuals? Are there any features that seem to be associated with success? What kinds of career do they have? In order to interpret their comments, which are extensively quoted in the remainder of this book, it is necessary for readers to have some picture of this selected group, and to recall that they are not necessarily representative of English teachers as a whole.

In many respects there was considerable variation. We had made it clear that those nominated could be of any age and could include those who were perceived as being particularly effective even if they were no longer classroom teachers. In the event (and predictably) virtually all were in the age-range 25 to 57; there were just one younger and one older than this, and the mean age was 39. Women accounted for 57 per cent, a rather smaller proportion than in the English-teaching profession as a whole, and gender differences are considered in more detail in a separate section of this chapter.

Details of the posts currently held indicated that something like three out of ten had moved on from teaching English full-time in schools, and now occupied related positions. Of these, eight were deputy heads, eight were advisory teachers, twelve had become advisers and six were lecturers. In view of the criticisms that are sometimes made of a supposed lack of classroom experience on the part of advisers and lecturers, it is worth noting that the mean length of classroom experience for the lecturers in our sample was over 13 years and for the advisers nearly 14. Rather over 10 per cent of the total sample were English teachers on the main professional grade, a slightly higher proportion held posts of responsibility for English, and 42 per cent were heads of English departments (including two teachers in their 20s). Virtually all had taught full-time in secondary schools, 15 per cent had also worked in primary schools, and significant numbers had experience in middle schools, tertiary colleges or in Further Education. A number had worked part-time, and the amount of full-time school teaching experience ranged from one year to thirty, with a mean of thirteen years. That experience had been gained in anything between one and nine schools, averaging about three schools for each teacher.

The great majority belonged to one or more organizations related to English teaching; only 16 per cent did not, and a fifth belonged or had belonged to two or more. The most striking finding here was that although various associations were mentioned by a few people (United Kingdom Reading Association, British Film Institute, the English Association and a variety of specialist groups for advisers or lecturers) one was absolutely dominant. Eighty-four per cent of the sample named membership of the National Association for the Teaching of English. Not all were uncritical of the Association, described by one as 'philosophy good, thinking woolly, practice vague'. Nevertheless, this high level of awareness and participation does seem to support views that the influence of that Association is disproportionate to the size of its membership, because it brings together so many of those who could be perceived as leading figures in the teaching of English.

The following sections of this chapter examine in more detail issues of qualification and gender, perceptions of significant influences and of the nature of English as a subject, career patterns and the supply of teachers.

Necessary qualifications

What does it mean to be qualified as an English teacher? Most of the arguments about entrants to the profession are based on the relative importance attached to the three elements: personality, academic achievement, and professional training. As suggested in Chapter 1, the earliest formulations tended to define English teachers largely in terms of the special personal qualities they should display. In part this was because there was no agreement at that time about what kind of academic qualification would be appropriate or about what kind of training (if any) they should be offered. Even as late as 1938 the Spens Committee concluded that professional training was unnecessary for grammar school masters, who would do better 'increasing their mastery of their special subjects, than in following a course in the University Training Department'.[1] Such views have emerged again recently, as will be seen in Chapter 4.

Our survey suggests that personal qualities remain the dominant consideration in the minds of English teachers themselves, as can be seen from their replies to the question, 'What seem to you the essential qualifications for someone who is going to become an effective English teacher?' Although 40 per cent mentioned areas of knowledge that candidates should have ('excellent knowledge of subject'; 'a good qualification in some aspect of English'; 'a good degree'; 'widely read'), the overall stress was on personal qualities, interests and attitudes. These areas accounted in all for 80 per cent of the criteria that were put forward. One deputy head teacher began his list of essential qualifications: 'Excellent intellect and outstanding personality!'

Teachers mentioned a wide range of personality traits, including (in no particular order) 'professionalism', 'charisma', 'enthusiasm', 'boundless energy', 'capacity for hard work', 'intelligence', 'inventiveness, open-mindedness', 'confidence', 'resilience', 'stamina', 'exuberance', 'sense of humour', 'sense of fun', 'playfulness', 'ingenuity', 'a lively imagination', 'a creative approach', 'a sense of vision', 'vitality', 'dedication and idealism', 'commitment', 'tough-mindedness', 'flexibility', 'adaptability', 'versatility', 'tolerance', 'fairness', 'approachability', 'compassion', 'sensitivity, sensibility and morality', 'wide human sympathies', 'infinite good humour', 'acting ability', and the possession of 'a thick skin'.

The ideal candidate would display 'real enjoyment' or 'delight' in the subject, be 'interested in language and in literature', indeed would show 'a passion for the subject', 'love of literature', 'lust for language' and 'have poetry at the heart' – the suppressed images are fascinating! In terms of English activities (and possessing 'a clear rationale' for them), an applicant 'should be a real reader and writer', must 'read a lot; write a lot; find language fascinating', have 'up to date knowledge of literary theory' and 'enthusiasm to keep abreast of current children's literature', be 'able to respond creatively to literature', 'able to communicate effectively', have 'a knowledge of English language structure' and 'linguistics', be 'able to inspire "real" writing in classrooms', take 'enjoyment in classroom research' and 'have an interest in such issues as gender and multiculturalism', taking care to display 'non-racist, non-sexist attitudes'. According to one, a good teacher is able 'to arouse interest in everything'!

Such a person would be 'an interactive teacher and sensitive to pupils' needs', would 'love pupils' (or 'like kids', according to one's preferred terminology), be 'committed to learning, not to teaching', 'able to relate to pupils as individuals', displaying 'genuine fondness of subject and children' and 'a fascination with how humans learn'. There would be the 'ability to cope with all ages and the whole breadth of ability', the 'ability to build strong personal relationships', to be 'inquisitive' and 'tolerant of noise in the classroom' but still be 'able to control a class'. Of many 'organizational skills', those most mentioned were 'classroom management', the 'ability to initiate and execute change', 'the capacity to get things in perspective', 'ability to work well with colleagues', 'ability both to perform and to integrate into a classroom', 'ability to listen responsively', being 'able to organize self and others', 'able to reflect, adapt and learn from mistakes'.

Such a sampling of generalized qualities indicates vividly the impossibility of drawing up any neat check-list that could be mechanically applied by those charged with selecting new entrants. Many of the named qualities would be unlikely to co-exist with others. Perhaps, as in examination papers, we should suggest: 'Attempt *not more than three* from each section'. As one adviser said, 'I have seen good English teachers of *all* kinds'. Some people suggested (not altogether light-heartedly) that essential qualifications might include 'a supportive partner', 'a flexible wardrobe' or a 'personable' appearance.

The actual paper qualifications held by those in our sample indicate clearly enough the variety of educational backgrounds from which English teachers come. If we look at our teachers' own academic and professional preparation, 13 per cent originally qualified with a teachers' certificate; 22 per cent with a BEd. degree; just over half held a BA or MA in English, normally (though not in all cases) followed by a PGCE; 12 per cent had first degrees in other subjects. There is a predictable relationship between age and the nature of the initial qualification. Whereas trained English graduates were of all ages throughout the range, those who began work with a teachers' certificate were almost all in their late 30s or older, and all the untrained graduates were over the age of 40. Those with BEd. degrees and those whose original degrees were in subjects other than English were almost exclusively in their mid-30s or 40s. The most recent DES statistics (April 1990) show that in 1989 those entering teaching were more or less equally divided between the BEd. route and the degree plus PGCE, but that the former was dominant for primary schools and the latter for secondary. Certainly the impression given by our sample is of narrowing entrance routes to an increasingly specialized profession, where an English degree plus a PGCE is becoming the norm for secondary teaching. As one argued, at least the possession of a good degree in the subject prior to training is one way of refuting those wearisome arguments about the supposed academic weakness of candidates.

Over half of the sample possessed additional qualifications, and this high proportion was another factor that distinguished our group from the profession in general. Some 17 per cent held advanced diplomas or certificates; 13 per cent had higher degrees in English and 26 per cent had higher degrees in education. There is some overlap here, because a few had acquired more than one such qualification, but it is also significant that of the 48 per cent who had not, a good number were at present engaged in taking advanced courses leading towards an award.

Gender differences

Teaching in general is commonly perceived to be 'women's work', and this applies with particular force to English teaching. Historical studies show that whereas in 1870 there were rather more male teachers in England than female, by 1930 women outnumbered men by nearly four to one.[2] The shift was even more extreme in the United States, emphasized by salary differentiation and by increasing opportunities for men outside teaching.[3] In the early 1980s, when women accounted for 40 per cent of university undergraduates, they supplied 70 per cent of those students in higher education involved in initial teacher education.[4] One follow-up study of women graduates found that 'most ended up as teachers, if not straight away, after a period of time in another occupation'.[5] The preponderance of women choosing to study English was also established early. From the eighteenth century onwards, literature in the vernacular had been advocated as a means to the social and moral education of girls, in place of the study of the classics offered to boys. Even before they were admitted as undergraduates at Oxford, women outnumbered men in English classes there and were generally felt to be more enthusiastic. English as a subject was more rapidly established in girls' schools, and the 1922 Committee concluded that 'in this subject the average achievement of girls was distinctly superior to that of boys'.[6] Over the last thirty years, the proportion of girls who were successful in English at A-level has risen to over 70 per cent of the total, and they account for a similar proportion of those on university degree courses in English (higher than in any other major subject except French).

It is hardly surprising, then, that women outnumber men as English teachers. What may be more surprising, in view of the figures above, is that the difference is not greater. The proportions of the sexes undertaking post-graduate training in English have remained virtually constant for twenty years: two women to every man. The proportion of women on BEd. courses is considerably higher. The most recent figures for secondary teachers show that those whose degree includes English as a subject (just under 20,000) are made up of 40 per cent men and 60 per cent women.[7]

Considering that women constitute the majority of English teachers, demographic studies suggest that they are significantly under-represented among teaching staff in university departments of education and in the advisory services. In our very small sample, 31 per cent of the male respondents were now working as advisers or lecturers, but only 7 per cent of the women (though this may in part be age-related, as more teachers in their 40s and 50s were men than women). More widely, studies of teaching at university level indicate that, across all subjects, women only account for 14 per cent of all full-time university staff (and only 2.7 per cent of professors), although – in a significant phrase – women are better represented in 'low-status fields such as education'.[8]

Our survey suggests that there are very few respects in which the perceptions of men and of women about the teaching of English are significantly different. At the beginning of their teaching careers, women felt that they were better prepared to teach drama and to work with children with special needs than men did. They were more likely than men to see the major obstacles to working as they wished as lack of time, stress and inadequate resources (whereas men were proportionately more likely to point to the imposed external pressures of government policies on the curriculum and assessment). In considering the distinctive qualities of English teachers, women were more likely than men to identify characteristic ways of working or to define attitudes like desire for autonomy, welcoming of change and 'progressiveness'. In no other cases were gender differences statistically significant.

Formative influences

How do English teachers come to be? We asked respondents to rank ten possible influences on a scale of one to five. The actual question was: 'How important and helpful in your development as a teacher do you consider each of the following to have been?' There were, of course, considerable differences in the rankings given to any item, depending on people's varied experiences, but none of the ten revealed any significant gender variation. It is probably simplest first to give the overall mean scores, arranged in order of their ratings with the highest first, and then to offer some commentary.

other English teachers	4.1
academic subject study	3.8
books or articles	3.7
membership of NATE or other organizations	3.5
heads of department	3.5
teacher training course	3.3
further academic study	3.2
in-service courses	3.1
English advisers	3.0
professional tutors in school	1.8

The first thing to note is the relatively limited range. If we exclude professional tutors, a relatively recent role, the other nine items are not widely separated. All had been generally of importance, and 'much' or 'great' importance to a good number of teachers. Perhaps the most interesting indication here is the high ranking given to the influence of other classroom English teachers, rather than those more usually seen as concerned with teacher development: heads of department, professional tutors or English advisers.

In certain respects these overall rankings require some commentary. It should be said, for example, that if we confine responses to 'further academic study' to those who have actually undertaken such work and thus speak from experience, the mean score would be 3.9, placing this item second in the rank order. Some significant differences can be attributed to age. If we look at the results, dividing those in their 20s and 30s from those in their 40s and 50s (remembering that the mean age of our sample was 39), a number of variations appear. Members of the younger group are much more likely to give a high ranking to their training than the older (3.6 as opposed to 3.0, with over double the proportion attributing much or great importance to this factor). There was an even more significant variation in attributing importance to heads of department, with the younger group's mean score at 3.8 as opposed to 3.1. By contrast, the older group attributed more importance to the influence of reading (3.9 mean as opposed to 3.3) and of further academic study.

The initial qualification of the teachers is another source of variation. Those with 'academic' degrees rated their experience of subject study rather more highly than those holding a teachers' certificate or BEd. degree. When considering teacher training courses, however, those with the BEd. recorded the highest mean rating for its importance, followed by those with a PGCE after a degree course, and with the teachers' certificate gaining the lowest rating. The importance of further academic study was given the highest rating by those with a certificate (4.3), followed by those with a BEd. (3.4) and those with a degree and

PGCE (2.8). Perhaps those who felt that their initial academic studies had been less helpful than they would have wished were particularly anxious to take further opportunities when they were available.

Reactions to the importance of books and articles are particularly interesting in attempting to suggest what has shaped teachers' thinking and practice. Just over half of the sample (57) said that reading had been of much or great importance in their development. They were invited to mention authors, books or articles that had been 'of particular importance' to them, and although some said that it was impossible to select from a great number, the majority did in fact name a few. The most significant observation concerns the variety of choice. Over 130 different items were mentioned and the variety may suggest something about the individualism of English teachers. One claims to have been significantly influenced only by works of literature, another lists Fish, Iser, Propp and Saussure, others mention *The Politics of Innovation*, *Teaching as a Subversive Activity* or *Grammatical Man*. Quantitatively, *English in Education* gets the most mentions, with readers from all age groups, and this is hardly surprising in view of the popularity of NATE which publishes that journal. *The English Magazine* and English Centre publications are also frequently named, proportionately more by younger teachers; *The Use of English* and *The Times Educational Supplement* occur rather less often. As far as particular authors are concerned, Douglas Barnes and David Holbrook were most cited, the latter exclusively by older teachers. Others picked out by five or more teachers are James Britton, Patrick Creber, John Dixon, David Jackson, Margaret Meek, Robert Protherough and Frank Smith. It would be dangerous to try to impose any pattern on such information, especially as several teachers commented that very different works had 'informed [their] thinking at various times' and had influenced them 'in very different ways'. We may suspect that English teachers (or, at least, effective ones) are more influenced by their reading than others are, but we lack comparative data to make this more than guesswork.

English teaching as a career

Can English teaching today be described as a worthwhile career? The responses of our group of teachers suggest a wide range of opinions. Asked what advice they would give to friends or to their own children who were thinking of becoming English teachers, they offered everything from warm encouragement to the direst warnings. In a nutshell, something like one in ten would offer strong support ('Do it! It's the most rewarding activity I know of') and an equal proportion strong discouragement ('Don't! Teaching is a job with built-in failure'). The great majority would qualify their recommendation ('yes, if ...' or 'no, unless ...'), or say 'it all depends on the person' (a response that was made proportionately much more by women than by men), or simply offer practical advice.

Age and length of experience accounted for no significant differences in atti-

tude, but there were marked variations according to the position currently held
and the initial training. Those who were classroom teachers of English were
more likely to advise against a teaching career than in favour of one (20 per cent
in favour, 25 per cent against). By contrast, those now serving as deputy heads,
advisers or lecturers were very much more positive (51 per cent in favour and
only 11 per cent against). This striking difference between those actually
engaged in full-time English teaching and the others may be related to the
dissatisfaction with career opportunities described later in this section. In
addition, those with BEd. degrees were markedly more likely to give negative
advice and less likely to give positive advice than those holding other initial
qualifications. This is one of several indications in the survey that those so
qualified are more dissatisfied than others.

In many cases there was a strong tug between past experience and views of the
present or future. One very experienced advisory teacher, a 'committed socialist'
who said 'all my happy teaching career was in state schools' and who 'would
happily have burned the independent schools', would now advise a prospective
teacher: 'Go into the independent sector where you can put more of your
energies into the subject itself' and 'where brilliant English teachers could
be rewarded for, and left alone to get on with, the effective teaching of English'.

There were similarly mixed responses to a question asking 'When people talk
of a "career" in English teaching, what do you see as the different stages (or
"rungs" in the "ladder")?' At one extreme were those who resisted the whole
'climbing' notion ('Can't think like that'; 'I don't see career in those terms') and
who said that they were 'suspicious' or 'sceptical' about those they regarded as
'career' teachers: 'They tend to be those most eager to get out of classrooms,
away from children and teaching situations'. One head of English demanded: 'Is
that the only way to think of a career? And I don't think about career much. To
develop *as an English teacher* you don't have to go up rungs'. An advisory teacher
who thought that 'English teachers are less ambitious than many others', said
that 'if they were allowed to concentrate undisturbed ... upon their teaching
they'd be happy to progress as increasingly effective teachers'. It has to be said,
however, that such idealistic views were expressed virtually exclusively by those
who were already in senior positions.

At the other extreme were those who lamented the lack of career opportunities
('at the moment there aren't any'; 'at present there are few', 'very little career
progress now': 'excellent teachers with experience have no chance of career
advancement'), and others who accepted the career ladder image but saw it as
inoperative at present: 'does such a thing exist?' or 'the rungs fall away as you
put your foot on them'.

What is the top of the ladder? For just under half of the group, mostly
younger teachers, it led to being head of department or faculty. For a quarter it
was to become an adviser or lecturer in teacher training and for one in seven to
become a deputy or head. How narrowly is 'a career in English' to be defined?
There were considerable disagreements between those who saw it as leading to

an advisory, training or management role and those who saw this as a change to something quite different: 'A "career" in English teaching comprises teaching English to children. Becoming head of department is a separate ladder including administration and management and in terms of English is irrelevant'.

What might account for such mixed feelings about their own profession and its career prospects? Few of the marks that would enable us to talk about a successful career in other fields seem to apply today to English teaching. There is little real sense of moving from grade to grade, each with its distinct title and salary scale. Nor is there much compensating indication (compared with professions like law or medicine) that, although one continues to practise and develop the same skills, the conditions, the esteem and the rewards improve with success. In the work they are expected to do and in the responsibilities they assume, teachers at the beginning of their careers are virtually indistinguishable from their more experienced colleagues. Increasing experience and expertise bring little in the way of greater opportunities, better conditions or increased rewards. As *The Handbook of Research on Teaching* puts it: 'Little premium is placed on cumulative mastery or professional initiative in a career that offers few rewards and opportunities based on evolving skill, sophistication and professional standing'.[9]

The problem was not so marked at a time when all the members of a secondary school staff, including the head, spent most of their time as subject teachers, when the 'senior' English master or mistress was just that, and when many were content to remain in one school for much of their teaching lives. Difficulties have been caused by the attempts to bolt on to the profession a managerial structure borrowed from industry. The separation of senior and middle 'management teams' and the increasing withdrawal of people with certain roles from teaching responsibilities have had a damaging effect. Teachers are well aware that the growing size of a school improves the salaries of heads and deputies, but not those of the head of English; that although senior teacher posts were intended to reward classroom expertise they have largely been hijacked by managers as a reward for administrative responsibilities.

The result has been a sense of mid-life crisis, as many of our respondents have pointed out: 'Once at head of department level you're stuck'. A lifetime spent in effective English teaching can come to look like failure. To enjoy what an outsider might call a successful career means giving up classroom teaching for administration, pastoral work or some other advisory or management function – 'In many respects a careerist is currently invited to cease being a teacher'. The irony is that the new role may not give the satisfaction of the old one, and it may not draw on the qualities that were associated with success in English teaching. 'I didn't come into teaching for *this*', said one dissatisfied individual. A head of English writes: 'No amount of expertise or flair in English teaching will get you promotion unless you take on management tasks which dilute the time you can give to your real *métier*'.

When asked what different post they would like to take up in the future, only one in ten heads of department in our sample named any position involving classroom work in English. They were very conscious that at this stage 'there are different ladders to climb', as one put it, 'gaining varieties of experience in a number of areas and then hoping for a different job'. Over a quarter of them aimed to become deputy heads, another quarter wished to be advisers or advisory teachers, one in ten wanted to work in teacher-training, 16 per cent would like to give up teaching for work in the arts or similar fields, and a number want administrative posts, other non-educational work or early retirement. It must surely be a matter for enormous concern that those perceived as being leaders of the profession have to envisage their careers in terms of giving up teaching English in school.

How does the situation look from the viewpoint of those who have actually made such a move? The responses of those who had changed from classroom English to English-related posts as lecturers, advisers or advisory teachers give no indications that any of them moved for the money, although one did say that he sought 'fame, wealth and leisure (none ensued)'. Their motives were almost all to do with the need for change and variety after years in school. One or two said candidly that they wanted 'to get out of schools', 'to avoid becoming Mr Chips' or to 'escape from a lunatic head teacher'. Advisory teachers, saying 'I wanted a change', 'a break from the classroom', suggested that teaching itself had become undervalued in the new managerial structures of their schools. From the viewpoint of the 'senior management team my own teaching was seen as being of little importance'; 'in school there were too many *unnecessary* administrative chores, above all too many unnecessary meetings'. For a number of these and for the advisers a change from teaching children to working with teachers seemed agreeable, and 'a natural progression' according to one.

Lecturers and advisers pointed frequently to 'wider experience', to greater 'autonomy of working practice' and to 'the opportunity to reflect' (or 'academic invigoration') as major motives for moving to their present positions. According to one, an effect of the change was 'ceasing to dislike myself for the things I'm forced to do'. Images of width and breadth extending beyond a single school were recurrent. They felt that they had gained 'a very wide view of English teaching', 'wider knowledge of the current state of English teaching', 'wider awareness of schools and of educational issues', 'a long-term perspective', 'a broader view of development', 'greater knowledge and understanding'. To quote one very experienced adviser, who had previously taught for fifteen years in three schools, the benefits of her post were: 'Much greater experience of a wide variety of schools and departments. Ability to see English in the whole-institution context. Greater understanding of the national situation and *much* increased political awareness'. There is a repeated sense of freedom from restrictions: 'no more acres of marking with no respite, no more responding to the bell'. Leaving the classroom meant 'time to think more about how people learn', 'more control of my work and a flexible timetable', 'more control over time (so that I could write more)'. What, by comparison, did they miss about work in schools? One said bluntly 'nothing' and another 'very little'. Most claimed to regret losing 'direct contact with pupils': 'the buzz of a good lesson and the immediate warmth of children enjoying English', 'unexpected delights (and debacles)', 'the unpredictable contributions and enthusiasms of pupils', the 'daily contact with young minds', 'the quality of children's achievements', 'the excitement of a good A-level group' because 'I still miss teaching A-level really badly'.

There may be a touch of sentimentality about these regrets but they also suggest that it is not the actual teaching of English that has prompted these individuals to move to other posts. Indeed, they still believe that they are contributing to that work, 'helping to bring about more enlightened English teaching', 'disseminating good practice', 'influencing teaching through initial training and in-service', 'revolutionizing the teaching of English' in a particular area, 'offering guidance', 'facilitating the exchange of ideas', 'participating in national projects', 'by publishing, by sitting on committees, trying to advance a view of English'.

These responses reinforce the view that the slump in teacher morale during the educational decline of the 1980s was less about money or status than about the way in which teachers' belief in themselves and in their work was eroded. Kenneth Baker and others succeeded all too well in making them feel guilty about themselves and about the work that they were doing (aided, it has to be said, by some equally ferocious Left-wing attacks on liberal-humanist models of English teaching). As will be apparent from the quotations above, our respondents overwhelmingly see themselves as men and women with a vocation, people who joined the English-teaching profession with a strong sense of altruism. In the 1980s it was fashionable to deride such motives; the language of morality and the imagination with concern for human values was squeezed out in favour of balance-sheet economics. In particular, there was persistent undermining of notions of professional expertise; it was the 'customers' and the 'clients' who were always right.

Over seventy years ago, Frank Roscoe wrote to deplore the low public esteem in which teaching was held, manifested in the 'meagre pittance' which teachers were paid and the lack of opportunities of 'gaining distinction'. Most of all, however, he stressed that young people with a sense of vocation should be afforded autonomy in their chosen profession. 'Excessive supervision and inspection will tend to discourage and eventually destroy that quality of initiative which is indispensable in all teaching'.[10] Studies of teachers suggest that their sense of professionalism is grounded at least as much in having individual control over their work and exercising responsibility as on such issues as hierarchical status or remuneration.[11] In the 1950s and 1960s, English teachers generally felt themselves free, within the bounds of professional responsibility, to make decisions about the curriculum, methods and assessment in partnership with one another and with other agencies charged with similar responsibilities. Recent governmental policy, however, has marked an abrupt change of direction.

In the absence of any professional body (such as the General Teaching Council in Scotland), the Secretaries of State for Education have vigorously employed powers that had previously gone unused. The emphasis now is on accountability and appraisal; it is managerial and bureaucratic rather than professional (a point that is further developed at the end of Chapter 3). Central control of the curriculum, imposed and standardized attainment tests, programmes of school and teacher evaluation and review, all reduce autonomy and compel the teacher to 'deliver' someone else's arbitrary package rather than making professional decisions in the interests of particular, known pupils. A parallel process has taken place in teacher education, where CATE criteria have been imposed on initial training and the powers of institutions to mount in-service courses have been undermined by financial and administrative changes. The rights of teachers and lecturers to participate in framing policy and making decisions in the fields of their own expertise have been severely curtailed; there has been a critical loss of control. In place of a cooperative, self-regulating learning community we now have pressures towards a hierarchical system with differential pay according to subject, 'incentives' for top managers recruited from outside the profession, and market-led competition between schools. The new model of managers making decisions which classroom operatives then implement has essentially de-professionalized teaching.

At the time of writing, it is too early to say what effects on career structures in English will be brought about by the coming of Local Management of Schools. It seems likely, however, that the results may be damaging. Any coordinated planning of career progression within a school becomes difficult when the financial pressure is towards appointing younger and cheaper English teachers and to using incentive allowances to retain teachers of other ('shortage') subjects. Recent research at the University of East Anglia suggests that the present career structure has trapped a quarter of the profession (mostly those who have been teaching between five and ten years) who remain unpromoted and increasingly disaffected.[12] Moving schools to gain promotion may become more difficult. If one becomes 'surplus to requirements' in a department, then the LEA can no longer guarantee a place elsewhere. The decision to remain 'where one is' is fast ceasing to be an option; because of the speed of change one can swiftly find oneself 'somewhere different', even though nominally one may have remained in the same post. It becomes increasingly difficult to separate out professional career choices from quite random external events (one year the LEA wants to retire everyone over 50; the next it wants to retire nobody) and from personal life-patterns (not pursuing promotion because it would mean moving one's children from a school where they are happy).

The once-lauded notion of professional detachment, total absorption in the career, no longer carries much conviction. English teachers who are called on to understand and to empathize with the lives and problems of their students will be particularly conscious of how thin the divisions are between personal and professional life. What teachers 'know about', the issues they can tackle, their views of texts, change as they marry, have children, divorce, go through the menopause, lose parents or loved ones, are seriously ill, get old, face retirement. The work does not look the same to a 24-year-old struggling back to a tiny flat with a pile of folders, to a mother trying to combine English teaching with bringing up two small children, or to a man in his 50s who has not gained promotion and is wondering whether to take early retirement. It is not just that they see what they are teaching differently; they have different relationships with their students. They are developing, they are 'making themselves' as English teachers, but they may doubt nowadays whether they have a 'career'.

The provision of English teachers

Questions of teacher supply and training have been notorious for political bungling and fudging, accompanied by piecemeal remedies that ignore the wider picture. A researcher of the future, reading the newspaper files, will be bewildered by the managerial incompetence displayed. In the 1960s, a desperate teacher shortage was met by tripling the output of colleges of education. Newspapers hailed 'a further welcome rise in the number of students training to be teachers' and the DES praised 'the hard thought, organisational ingenuity, pioneering attitudes, additional work and some inconvenience' which had brought this about.[13] Few of those who had put in the hard work and suffered the inconvenience realized that they had done their work all too well, and that the whole mechanism was to be flung into reverse.

By the end of the 1960s, problems of over-expansion, particularly in the light of a falling birth-rate, were known and conveyed to the James Committee, but the figures were never published by them or by the then Secretary of State for Education, Margaret Thatcher. Within a decade, the number of students enrolling for concurrent courses in the public sector was cut by five-sixths (from 45,600 students in 1971 to 8,700 in 1980). The first peremptory cuts in target numbers were announced in 1973, greeted by articles headed 'Agony of the colleges' and 'Thoughtless destruction'. By 1975 it was 'Colleges axed', followed a year later by 'Thirty more training colleges face axe', and then 'Government axes more training colleges'.[14] The whole programme lacked any coherence as targets were given and revised at breakneck speed. No criteria for the cuts and closures were ever put forward.

The irony is that even at this time teaching was already appearing less attractive as a career, and the treatment of the colleges simply confirmed this judgement in the minds of possible candidates. There were the first indications that 'Top teachers are quitting schools'[15] in a survey from the Economist Intelligence Unit. As for new entrants, in 1969–70 the numbers going to colleges of education dropped for the first time in ten years. The accelerating trend (1975 was the lowest level for three years) did not only apply to the colleges. In 1973 the first drop in applications for post-graduate training since 1966 was recorded, and in 1974 applicants for one-year graduate courses were down by 19.5 per cent. Significantly, English and science were the two worst affected subjects and applications from men were down by 26 per cent.[16] The stark fact is that the cuts and the panics – '10,000 new teachers heading for the dole'[17] – caused problems rather than solving them. Far from having too many recruits, the country attracted too few, as potential teachers read the discouraging signs. The new, low recruitment targets for 1978 were not met, leaving 'the polytechnics struggling to fill their places', and already the headlines were 'shortage of teachers forecast'.[18] When by 1984 the Advisory Committee on the Supply and Education of Teachers told Sir Keith Joseph that 46,000 extra teachers would be needed by 1993, he discounted their advice and wound up the Committee. The members of the Committee have, of course, been proved right.

From the middle of the 1980s onwards the news has been consistent: 'desperate shortage', 'devastating fall in applications', 'English graduates target unlikely to be met', 'Heads alarmed at training shortfall', 'Shock fall in standard of recruits', 'Shortage fears grow', 'Shortage problem worsening – HMI'.[19] Perhaps the oddest feature of the whole lamentable affair has been the continuing pretence by the DES and the government that there is no problem. Mrs Angela Rumbold did not find an audience of head teachers persuaded by her insistence that recruitment difficulties were a 'myth'.[20] Only in December 1988 was the government forced by the Commons select committee on education to admit that there might not be enough teachers to deliver the National Curriculum.[21] Leaders of industry and head teachers made 'sharp criticisms of the Department of Education and Science for misplaced optimism and inadequate methods of defining targets'.[22] The number of trained teachers entering secondary schools in 1989 was only three-quarters of the total for 1984. In addition, only a third of those who enter training still remain in the profession after five years. The teaching unions suggested that permanent vacancies in schools were 'twice as severe as the government's estimates' and that a quarter of secondary staff were actively planning to leave; research at Manchester University claimed that five times more teachers were leaving the profession than official statistics reveal.[23] Her Majesty's Inspectors have been forthright: Mr Eric Bolton said that 'supply is the crucial question over the next ten years' and foresaw a threat to the quality of education that would imperil the heart of the Education Reform Act. 'Standards of learning are never improved by poor teachers, and there are no cheap, high quality routes into teaching'.[24]

Within this wider picture, the situation of English teaching gives rise for particular concern. DES statistics show that, as part of the general increase in graduate teachers, the number of teachers with English as the first subject of their degree rose between 1971 and 1986, but the size of this increase (44 per cent) was markedly less than that for some other subjects. Over the same period there was, for example, an increase of more than 50 per cent in mathematics and in physics. Whereas in 1971 English accounted for 16 per cent of all graduates in teaching, by 1986 the proportion had shrunk to 9 per cent.

In view of all the loose talk about 'shortage subjects' it is perhaps worth noting that in the last full year (1986) for which figures are available at the time of writing, only 20 per cent of English teachers hold an honours degree in their subject, as compared with 25 per cent in physics, 31 per cent in biology, 35 per cent in chemistry and 36 per cent in French. Between 1983 and 1986, while the number of specialist graduate teachers in secondary schools increased overall, there was an actual decrease in the number with English as a degree subject (contrasted with an increase in mathematics). Similarly, the annual figures of unfilled teaching places in maintained secondary schools show that English vacancies are only exceeded by those for mathematics (and the DES staffing survey of 1988 predicts that in the mid-1990s there will actually be a surplus of maths teachers). There are more than twice as many unfilled English posts as physics ones (and four times as many English vacancies as ones in chemistry). In the period 1981 to 1987, while there has been a decrease in the annual vacancies for mathematics, physics, chemistry or French, the number of vacancies in English has risen (doubling between 1985 and 1990).

The chief reason for this is clear. For every ten English graduates accepted for secondary training in 1980, there were only six in 1986. This was in part a reflection of university cuts in the subject: in 1986 the number of undergraduates studying English was only 85 per cent of the 1980 total. Still more, however, it showed the dual effect of government restrictions on recruitment and of young people's increasing disillusionment with teaching as a career. University figures indicate that the proportion of English graduates proceeding to teacher training decreased abruptly between 1980 and 1986, from 12.8 per cent of the total to 6.32 per cent. Everyone within the profession has known for years that there is a desperate shortage of suitably qualified English teachers. They know it from anecdotal evidence about the difficulty of filling posts, as well as from the statistics and from the evidence in a series of reports like *A Language for Life* (The Bullock Report) or the HMI *Secondary Survey*. The 1988 staffing survey shows the continuing 'suppressed' or 'hidden' shortage (in DES-speak) of English teachers, whereby a quarter of those teaching the subject are unqualified. The latest HMI survey of secondary English in Wales reported that only one in twelve English lessons was taught by a suitably qualified specialist and that only a third of those teaching the subject had a good honours degree including English.[25] Despite this evidence, there has been a protracted attempt by government to pretend that this situation does not exist, that English is not a shortage subject. The next two chapters, dealing with the initial professional preparation of English teachers, must be read with this fact in mind.

3　The preparation of English teachers

The wider debate over teacher education

This book is being written as 'a wave of criticism has been breaking over the country's teacher-trainers', at 'a time of unprecedented questioning of teacher education, and the questions extend to whether it has a future at all in anything like its present institutionalized forms.'[1] Some of the concerns about traditional courses of preparation are conveniently summarized in the opening paragraphs of the chapter by Davies and Benton. The last decade has seen a series of over-lapping proposals for regulating, relocating or even abolishing the system, and the actual or potential effects of these on the preparation and careers of English teachers must be considered. This chapter looks briefly at the way in which initial 'training' for English teachers originated and then examines the views of our group of teachers about the preparation they received at varying times in the past. It considers some of the problems faced by those at present charged with the education of English teachers, concluding with a discussion of the effects of recent government policy. Chapter 4 examines the opinions of our group and of others about how the system of pre-service education might be changed. The following chapters, 5 to 8, then reflect on some different modes of teacher education that are currently being practised, written by people directly involved in the process.

The beginnings of teacher education in English

How did ideas of appropriate training begin to emerge? The first chapter examined the ambiguous attitudes towards English specialism in the Newbolt Report. Its chapter on the training of teachers begins firmly enough:

> The improvements in the teaching of English which we hope to see can only be brought about through a steady influx of teachers whose own training in English has been liberally conceived and carried out. (Para. 159)

What kind of 'training' did the Committee have in mind? And where was the 'steady influx' to come from? At the time, the actual situation was bleak. A significant proportion of teachers in elementary schools were wholly unqualified or only partly qualified, and 'we seem bound to accept [this] for the time being'. The Report expressed hopes that more selected students might be able to make a special study of English in a third year in college (184), but concentrated particularly on the expansion of demand at university: 'We look forward to a large increase in the students of English at the Universities owing to the importance and attraction of the subject itself' (212).

In this respect, at least, their hopes were more than justified. Three years later, progress was defined 'notably by the development of the English Honours Schools at the universities – the main source of supply of teachers competent to undertake the teaching of the higher forms'.[2] The Board also welcomed the increasing interest of universities in the training of teachers, particularly through the provision of courses in university training departments after a degree, because 'only under such conditions ... can teachers be fully grounded and confirmed in the idea of a liberal education'. Two-year training was hardly adequate; 'we look forward to a time when a really large proportion of our elementary school teachers will be persons who have completed a full University training'. Incidentally, it is interesting to note that at this time much of the methodology seems to have been school-based. 'At Cambridge, for instance, students who wish to be specially trained in English teaching are placed under the personal supervision of the chief English Master at the Perse School, and are virtually "trained" by him'. Ultimately, if the teaching of English was to be lifted to a 'higher level', then courses for serving teachers would be necessary.[3]

In these respects, England lagged behind the United States, where five-year and six-year patterns of teacher education had existed since 1917[4] and where the Hosic Report of that year had demanded that novices and non-specialists 'must give way to the professional':

> The supreme essential to success in high-school English is the trained teacher – the teacher trained by the study of his [sic] subject, by the study of educational principles and methods, and trained by experience.[5]

How 'professional' in the first two of these three respects did our respondents feel that their initial preparation, undertaken at various times between the 1950s and the 1980s, had been?

Teachers' views of their training

Historically, a change in teachers' experiences of training and their attitudes towards it is very strongly suggested in the responses of our group. Asked in general terms how important and helpful they felt their teacher-training had been, those in their 50s were the group most likely to reply 'little or none'. Such a judgement was less common among those in their 40s, less common still among those in their 30s and least common of all with those in their 20s. Putting it another way, six out of ten of those under 40 said their training had been 'much' or a 'great' help to them, as compared with only about a quarter of those aged 40 or over. It should perhaps be added that although there is not a necessary correlation between age and length of service, only one of the over-40s had trained at all recently, and that one had found the course helpful.

A more detailed picture is given in replies to a question asking how well people felt they had been prepared in just over twenty different respects when they began teaching. In the majority of cases there was a statistically significant difference between the replies of the under-40s and the over-40s. Such a difference was highly predictable in areas which training might not have tackled some years ago: the use of information technology, teaching English in a multi-cultural society or non-sexist teaching. However, the differences extended well beyond such areas, as examples can illustrate.

Compared with the older teachers, the younger were twice as likely to say that when beginning teaching they had felt well or very well prepared for classroom work with novels and stories, for encouraging poetry reading and writing, and for classroom management and control. They were four times more likely to say that they were well or very well prepared to organize and encourage talking and listening, to plan coherent programmes of work and to teach across the whole ability range. They were seven times more likely to have felt well prepared for the management of small group work. The only area where older teachers rated their preparedness more highly than younger ones was 'knowledge of English language structure'.

Looking at topics where teachers felt almost wholly *un*prepared, the older were at least twice as likely to name media studies, keeping records of children's progress, and working with children with special needs. The differences in perceptions were less striking in drama, in encouraging and marking written work, in book selection, in understanding and aiding children's language development, and in preparing classes for assessment at 16+. In these cases also, though, the mean ranking for preparedness was higher in the younger group than in the older. The only items where age did not seem a discriminator were A-level teaching and library work. There does seem evidence here to support the view that over the years courses of training have been perceived by students as increasingly effective and professional in preparing them for their role as English teachers. The Inspectorate has similarly reported on the fact that a higher proportion of new teachers felt satisfied with their training in 1987 than in 1981, and that in some aspects the improvement was 'very marked'.[6] Certainly those who trained relatively recently seem much more likely to feel that they were adequately prepared.

Which aspects of preparation for English teaching were perceived as being most effective? Ranking the reactions of our sample as a whole to twenty-two areas, they felt themselves best prepared for major aspects of the English curriculum (the top three items were 'classroom work with novels and stories', 'encouraging and marking written work' and 'encouraging poetry reading and writing') and for planning and organizing their work ('classroom management and control' actually came fourth, followed by 'planning coherent programmes of work' and 'teaching across the whole ability range'). They felt least well prepared for working with children with special needs, for non-sexist teaching and for the use of information technology, but older respondents pointed out that such areas had 'not been thought of' when they trained!

It would be dangerous to read too much into generalizations of this kind. They record the perceptions of effective teachers, and those who are less successful would probably report differently (about classroom management and control, say). For each of the topics named above, some teachers in the sample felt that they had been well prepared and others said that their preparation was poor or non-existent. There is also an interesting tension between this rough measure of effective preparation and another question asking about the major *omissions* in teachers' preparatory courses. What had they particularly missed? High up on the list, mentioned by approximately one out of five, were 'teaching across the ability range' and 'planning programmes of work', closely followed by 'classroom management and control' – three of the topics relatively *highly* rated for effectiveness of preparation. Indeed, only 'understanding children's development in English' was picked out more often than these three items as a major omission. How is this to be explained? It may simply be that these were areas that differentiated strongly between courses that dealt well with the subject and those that largely ignored it. Alternatively, perhaps these responses indicate a difference between those topics where preparation left teachers feeling able to cope and those where teachers still felt vulnerable despite the coverage that had been given; a distinction between aspects that could to some degree be generally mastered in advance and those that could really only be acquired on the job in particular situations.

It is hardly surprising that very few felt that their courses had lacked attention to the curricular areas of English: teaching fiction, work with poetry, dealing with writing, and examination work. The omission of some other topics was not generally seen as serious. Although respondents in general felt unprepared for working with the media, for school library work or for non-sexist teaching, very few named these as significant. The closest relationship between relative unpreparedness and regret at this omission was recorded about 'working with children with special needs' and 'use of information technology in English', followed by 'keeping records of children's progress'.

Finally, one specific example of the conflict between general attitudes and intense personal feelings may be helpful. The great majority of teachers in the survey said they felt ill-prepared for 'teaching English in a multi-cultural society', but fewer than one in ten saw this as a 'major omission'. Within this general pattern, however, there were some who identified this as an essential element in training and one that needed to be redefined. A secondary teacher wrote strongly:

> *All* students and teachers should be made aware of *racial issues* in teaching, rather than undergoing courses in multi-cultural education. There is a huge difference. As

a black woman entrant into teaching, my own awareness two years ago was so limited that I was favourably impressed by the popularity of 'multi-cultural' literature (e.g. *East End at your Feet*, etc.) and by its ever-growing use in schools. However, English teachers suffer from the same (curable!) affliction as others in this area: a multi-cultural text becomes an excuse for tinkering on the surface, the wheeling out of liberal platitudes, e.g. *Sumitra's Story* ('Actually I've done my anti-racist homework and I know Asian girls really like arranged marriages – I'd love to have one myself!') – in short, the 'saris, steel bands, samosas' approach; no analysis of the issues.... Also, study more high-level texts, e.g. Naipaul, Rushdie, Walcott, Angelou, Walker, etc., and give 'multi-cultural' literature *status*.... I have the confidence now to teach in a more anti-racist rather than patronising 'multi-cultural' way, e.g. I will correct Asian pupils if they make grammatical mistakes that will prevent them from achieving highly.

Problems for teacher-educators

Below all the immediate difficulties facing those charged with planning (or, in current jargon, 'delivering') programmes of teacher education in English lurk two enduring problems. The first is the conflict of different expectations. Government, schools, universities, business interests, local authorities, parents and children themselves all define what they want in different and frequently irreconcilable terms. The second is the low status which is afforded to teacher education in general and to English in particular. A consideration of these two problems leads into a section examining the effects of recent government policy.

Conflicting priorities are revealed in the contrasting aims that are embedded in different models of the process. Different views of desirable teacher preparation (or education, or training) have always existed along a continuum between two poles, the theoretical and the practical, the academic and the vocational. Those of us who prefer to talk of 'teacher *education*' tend to see the process as one in which the acquisition of knowledge, understanding and experience brings about changes in the person undergoing that process (an argument further developed by Anthony Adams in his chapter). Those who habitually talk of 'teacher *training*' emphasize the acquiring of competence in specific vocational skills and abilities. At one end there is the feeling that education, like architecture or medicine, is a serious study; that practical knowledge and skill must be accompanied by deeper professional understanding of principles. In this respect, the situation of English teaching has been mirrored in the preparation for other vocations, particularly those in fields like social work and the arts, where the deployment of skills cannot be separated from the unique personal qualities of the practitioner.[7] At the other end comes the apprenticeship view of teaching as a skill acquired by practice that almost anybody with a grasp of the appropriate subject matter can do. At its most extreme such a view holds that nobody can be *taught* how to teach. Teacher educators have long been assaulted from both extremes, caricatured on the one hand as peddling irrelevant facts about the history of education and on the other as offering low-level tips for teachers.

There is a second (and less understood) division, between those who wish the process to be essentially conservative, concerned to fit teachers for schools as they now are, able to fit swiftly into the classroom, and those who feel that institutions should be innovative, feeding new methods and materials into the schools, preparing student-teachers to live with change, able to develop effectively in the future. This in turn is related to a third (and currently much discussed) distinction between the relative importance of individualism and conformity, at both the personal and the institutional levels. Is the role of the training institution to encourage students to develop their own personal teaching styles, to become different people, or to move towards some kind of accepted 'teacher' norm? Should the college or department have its own particular strengths and emphases, or should it conform to some centrally agreed list of criteria? Different groups hold opposed opinions about each of these three issues.

At present, the need to please irreconcilable forces is seen particularly clearly in university schools of education. They are simultaneously in the hands of the DES (which allocates student numbers) and of CATE (which validates their courses), of their universities (whose policies govern their resources, staffing and promotion) and of the LEAs and schools (whose in-service budgets largely determine what advanced and short courses can be offered). Individual lecturers are expected to be at once scholars, practitioners and trainers. Thus in their careers they are required to compete in terms of research and publication with colleagues in academic departments who do not have to teach time-consuming method sessions, or to work in schools, or to be in favour with the local authority. Despite the good relations that exist in some institutions between those in education and colleagues in English or in other academic departments, the feeling still exists that education is the poor relation.

The second major problem is that teacher education has always been a much-criticized and undervalued part of the wider education system. The reasons for this are clear. It is a relatively small part of that system, training people for a single vocation and thus vulnerable to external pressures from government and bureaucrats. The low status attributed to teaching itself as a profession (partly because it deals with children rather than with adults and has no choice about who the clients will be) is associated with the training process, and it is all too easy to blame the shortcomings of schools and teachers on the preparation they received.

Historically, not only were those being trained for elementary schools of low academic attainment and drawn from the lower social classes, they were also given an inferior education that would not feed their social ambitions.[8] The staff of the colleges 'were not distinguished by their qualifications or accomplishments', and in some cases had no practical school teaching experience themselves.[9] Although the pattern of a three year degree course followed by a year of professional training was embodied in the regulations of 1913, it was half a century before that training became fully established. Such beginnings have tended to colour what followed. A disdain for what was perceived as low-level teacher education was marked in higher education, where an ability to teach has never been a major criterion either in making appointments or in offering promotion. In his lively and perceptive account of university specialists in modern languages, Colin Evans remarks sardonically that it is 'fatal' to think of oneself as a teacher of the subject, because 'the pure teaching activity is suspect'. Universities operate 'a peer culture which rewards researchers and ignores teachers'; 'teachers, even very good teachers, cast a short shadow (and are never promoted)'.[10] To teach potential *school* teachers places one at an even lower level of esteem: 'There is an inverse relationship between professional prestige and the intensity of involvement with the formal education of teachers'.[11]

Most university staff, in the United States as well as in Britain, resisted the establishment of education departments (just as they earlier resisted the introduction of English), arguing that from their standpoint there was no such subject as 'Education'. Even when teacher education became accepted, it remained a poor relation. It was marginal to the academic pattern of undergraduate courses, and academics who were themselves untrained as teachers ('gifted amateurs ... just thrown into it'[12]) were dubious about the value of such work. It was said in the 1940s that 'the bulk of academic opinion has had no real belief in teacher training and has been half ashamed of the university's part in it'.[13] Responses of university teachers suggest that in part this attitude is a defensive cover. If lecturers' own teaching is not effective and is criticized by students, then it may be easier to call the missing skills trivial than to set about acquiring them.[14]

Furthermore, as Tony Becher has pointed out, education suffers in academic valuation because it does not fit neatly into the conventional pattern of 'disciplines', being vocationally oriented, with overlapping professional and academic responsibilities, dealing with people rather than with objects and confronted with ever-changing problems and solutions.[15] In his conclusion, Becher tellingly points out how education ranks low in estimates of academic research, because criteria are applied which pre-determine that judgement, favouring supposedly 'pure' and 'objective' projects 'because they seem to lend themselves to simple and uncontentious measurement as against complex and contestable judgement'.[16]

Teacher educators (significantly overlooked as a group in most studies of teacher education) experience significant differences from other academics in recruitment and career patterns. To work in English in education, a lecturer will have to have spent a significant period of time as a successful school teacher, and will thus enter the university system much later than others. Such a person's qualifications will be professional as well as academic, and should include an ability to work well with students (a criterion which seems largely ignored in appointing other academic staff). According to Fuller and Bown, the supervisory responsibilities in education are more demanding than in any other form of professional training, let alone in orthodox academic departments.[17] Because of the outside demands and because staff in education almost all have responsibility for particular sub-areas, the administrative and committee load is greater than in other university departments, and the tension between different roles is greater. Far from being rewarded for the extra burdens, education staff are less well treated in terms of promotion than other academics.

Government policies for teacher education

It would be impossible to discuss this subject without considering the effect of government policies. After years of arms-length treatment, political and demographic shifts have led to an increasingly interventionist attitude by central government. The authors of this book have lived through unprecedented changes, in which huge increases in teacher training numbers 'in the national interest' were rapidly followed by closures and mergers, also 'in the national interest' (described in Chapter 2). Skilled men and women were pulled out of schools to work shifts (cheerily known as Box and Cox) in split-site institutions, only to be pressured a few years later into taking early retirement. Now we are approaching another period in which expansion is being called for. Boom and bust decisions are always made too late, despite the clear demographic evidence, in panic ways that negate proper planning. What is more, policies are increasingly being framed and decisions being taken on the basis of hunch or prejudice.

The White Paper *Teaching Quality* (1983) and DES circulars of 1983 and 1984, *Initial Teacher Training: Approval of Courses* marked the final abandonment of the principle that the government would simply act on professional advice. The White Paper was vague and misty about what that 'quality' might be but was hard and doctrinaire in asserting the measures that were supposed to achieve it – whatever it was. 'The government intends' recurs like a refrain; there is no concern for evidence or supporting rationale. These documents embodied the particular whims of Sir Keith Joseph. He set up and nominated the members of the Council for the Accreditation of Teacher Education, gave them their brief and charged them to report directly to him. The whole of this process was based on a series of assumptions which were implied or asserted without supporting arguments.

At the most basic level, it was simply assumed that improving teacher quality was to be achieved by regulating initial training (rather than, perhaps, by better in-service education, or by improving the quality of recruitment by better pay and conditions). In recruitment, it was assumed that graduates in those subjects that occur in the school curriculum were 'appropriate' and that others were not (and this had particular implications for English, where PGCE groups had frequently and deliberately drawn on occasional specialists in linguistics, psychology or sociology alongside English graduates). It was assumed that selection processes would be improved by using classroom teachers to interview candidates, that extending the length of the academic year (but not extending it to two years) and increasing the periods spent in school would improve performance, and that 'recent and relevant' school experience was essential for teacher-trainers (though not, apparently, for advisers, inspectors, head teachers or the Secretary of State for Education). However apparently respectable, all these assumptions were unproved, and some of them ran against what research evidence there was.[18] No consideration was given to providing additional resources to bring about the proposed changes, or to the staffing implications, or to how courses might be assessed, or to the links between initial training, induction and in-service development.

The Council for the Accreditation of Teacher Education is not a professional or representative body; it consists of those nominated by the Secretary of State for Education, and we look forward with interest to what will happen when there is a change of government. Labour's educational plans, just like Conservative ones, assert that 'teacher training must be reformed' and promise a 'student teacher core curriculum',[19] but with little indication of what those reforms or that curriculum might look like. At present, the lauded independence of Her Majesty's Inspectors has been dangerously compromised by making the reports on their visits to universities (with the polite fiction that these are by invitation, of course) obligatory for course approval by CATE. In fact, many of us are grateful for the support offered by members of the Inspectorate, but that need not be tied to their regulatory role.

The establishment of the Council in 1984 was only one in a series of measures and documents concerned with teacher education in that decade. Not only were the Council's criteria for the approval of courses founded on no solid evidence, it is even more significant that no research programme was ever established to appraise the Council's influence. We feel that in some ways there have been beneficial effects, and that some institutions have gained from the need to re-examine their courses. On the other hand, to consider reports from Her Majesty's Inspectors and other official bodies alongside the demands of the DES indicates how confused and contradictory some of the CATE requirements were.

All the demands for better and expanded courses were accompanied by the proviso that no additional resources would be available, despite the evidence in government reports of a clear relationship between better resources and better standards in schools (and the targeting of under-resourcing as one of the major causes of problems for new teachers in schools). 'Partnership' between schools and universities was demanded, but with no indication of how this might be organized and paid for. A better 'match' between teachers in training and the needs of the education service was proclaimed, but the sole body with expertise in this area, the Advisory Council for the Supply and Education of Teachers, was abolished. The scheme for 'enabling' lecturers to return to the classroom for a term has benefited schools more than it has the trainers or their institutions, according to the Inspectorate,[20] and Anthony Adams is only one of a number to find it 'largely a waste of time'. Complaining that training institutions were too traditional and unwilling to change, CATE then packaged the curriculum for them in the most traditional of terms, even specifying the minimum number of hours that should be spent on particular subjects. Most paradoxical of all has been the espousal of a free market economy (the values of which are to be conveyed in all training courses) combined with the total abandonment of this principle in the rigid application of target numbers for different subjects and institutions.

The new and 'permanent' CATE established in 1989 by DES circular 24/89 seems to wish to control both input and output: it still legislates for the contents of courses, laying down the number of hours to be devoted to particular topics, but also lists the desirable competences that are meant to be achieved by students. These are couched in the usual DES-speak to sound unexceptionable but to prove slithery in application. In English, the only behavioural objectives that can be manifestly displayed and assessed are the essentially low-level ones like writing legibly on a blackboard or framing effective questions. Most of those that are mentioned, like understanding 'the different ways in which pupils develop and learn', are not absolutes to be mastered by the end of a course but abilities that teachers go on developing throughout their lives. What *degree* of understanding is to be expected? In addition, if competences are to be demonstrated, they will have to be shown in very variable classroom conditions. The ability to ensure 'that work is carried out in a responsible and orderly manner' may come easily in one school without necessarily predicting equal success in another. Some of the problems associated with turning such statements into 'profiling' are picked out by Anthony Adams in his chapter.

Most crucially of all, the CATE document makes no attempt to distinguish between those competencies that are essential for all teachers beginning their careers and those that are more marginal or fashionable; all are listed at the same level. It is ironic that Sir Keith Joseph's desire to eliminate what he called 'clutter' from training programmes should have resulted in yet more of it, including items that would be more sensibly developed during a properly structured induction. At the same time there are some glaring omissions. Industrial understanding and knowledge of the legal framework are named as apparently essential, but not the capacity to reflect on educational issues, to plan sequential programmes of work, to work as one of a team within an English department, to prepare and use appropriate resources or to establish a personal teaching style and subject philosophy. The notion that by working in this way one can make a blueprint of an effective English teacher and then mass-produce examples of such a paragon is a delusion.

4 How might English teachers be made?

Looking forward

Having looked at the past and the present, it is now time to look forward. The real question is not whether teacher education should be improved (as all human activities need to be better) but *how*? What might the preparation of English teachers look like in the 1990s and beyond? Is there a world beyond CATE? It has become fashionable to use vague complaints about the existing system in order to propose that we need different paths into the profession. Michael Fallon, the schools minister, claims that 'We have already broken the monopoly of the teacher training colleges, and that is the key to change'.[1] Quite apart from noting his quaint idea that preparation still goes on in places called teacher training colleges and his odd application of the word 'monopoly', we may be intrigued to know what improvements his 'key to change' will unlock. This chapter examines some of the proposals currently being canvassed with most enthusiasm.

Teachers' views of 'ideal' preparation

How did our group of respondents feel that 'ideally' English teachers should be trained? One replied sardonically 'very well indeed', but left unsaid how that was to be achieved. Overwhelmingly, however, they were in favour of extended pre-service preparation, although their views on how this might best be achieved varied considerably. By contrast, only one mentioned the Articled Teacher scheme as a possible basis, and nobody advocated the Licensed Teacher route. Although they were not uncritical of the teacher education programmes they themselves underwent, the great majority still envisaged 'ideal' preparation in terms of a degree and PGCE course or of a BEd., particularly the former. A number would advise prospective entrants to take a PGCE course at particular (sometimes named) universities, adding such comments as 'my own post-grad. course (while it had omissions) was excellent' or 'a PGCE is essential'.

Although one person felt that a twelve-week introductory course might be sufficient, equally divided between 'short intensive courses' on 'drama, practical classroom control and poetry/story/play writing', followed later by a 'post-mortem at the end of the first or second year of teaching', the most common suggestion for improvement was to extend the length of the PGCE course. Many echoed those young teachers surveyed recently by the Inspectorate, who found their courses 'well balanced and useful', but felt that the chief constraint was lack of time.[2] They wanted 'the PGCE to be extended', a course of 'at least two years after a degree', 'a PGCE over two years, more *theory* and more *practice*', or a five-year period of preparation. One typical reply was: 'I would prefer to see a longer PGCE with an increased amount of classroom experience in which time was available for practising teachers and university lecturers to work alongside students'. Those who are actually teaching and receiving new teachers into their schools give no support to those radical critics who wish to sweep away any national system of teacher education (discussed in the final section of this chapter).

Among the general references to the relationship between schools and training institutions were indications of a mounting feeling that schools should assume a greater role than in the past. While only about one in ten thought that ideally schools alone should have this responsibility, and the great majority believed in some form of 'partnership', more of them favoured a relationship weighted towards the schools than an equal or university-dominated pattern. We antici-pated that enthusiastic and effective English teachers would be anxious to take a larger share in teacher education, especially as many of them already had considerable experience as teacher-tutors for colleges and departments of education. However, written and oral responses reveal rather hazy notions about how the schools might extend their share of training. There is repeated expression of the idea that trainees should work 'alongside' experienced teachers, or that schools should adopt the 'apprenticeship model' currently favoured by Right-wing theorists, or that students should 'shadow' and be 'on the job with the HOD'. It remains unclear just how trainee teachers would 'work alongside' and how the mentor's teaching and training responsibilities would be reconciled. Very few respondents make more precise suggestions or consider the timetabling problems. They say, for example, that students should observe 'a variety of teaching styles', that they should learn to 'team-teach', that their classroom time should be 'more structured' and have 'proper support', that they should be monitored and helped by 'professional tutors with *real* time to tutor', that both tutor and trainee should be given 'one-third timetables to have time to plan and evaluate'. This clear but largely unfocused support for schools as the dominant partners in initial training seems to arise in some responses both from a mistrust of lecturers' understanding of education 'as it really is' and from the familiar view of training that polarizes practical experience and 'theory', putting the emphasis on the former.

Among a minority there is a discernible groundswell of discontent that those in universities and colleges have, in some respects, different responsibilities and interests from those in schools. Several suggest that a lecturer's chief qualification should be closeness to the classroom. 'Students should be trained by English teachers of today *not* by college tutors who haven't taught for twenty years'; 'they should have training by *recent* ex-heads of department', 'by teachers who have themselves been responsible for good practice (these teachers serving only a short time away from the classroom – the longer away the more useless the advice)'. It is ironical that a number of these teachers express elsewhere career ambitions to become lecturers in education departments, where they presumably would become regarded in their turn as out of touch.

Experience of academic research, required by lecturers' contracts, is perceived by one respondent as counter-productive rather than enabling. 'If lecturers are going to remain credible they've got to cease thinking about their latest arcane article in the *Journal of Educational Policy* and prove their credibility at street level'. In other words, lecturers are only acceptable if they are virtually indistinguishable from classroom teachers. What is the point, though, of asking university tutors to do what teachers in their own classrooms can obviously do better?

The majority, and particularly the more experienced teachers, believed that school teachers and tutors bring different and complementary characteristics to the training 'partnership' (a word frequently used, although questioned in the Cambridge chapter of this book). All of those who have written for this volume believe in some form of 'fruitful collaboration', an effective 'division of roles' that is mutually supportive and illuminating, 'genuine links' between people as well as between institutions, expressed in 'different working relationships'. Tutors, for example, should 'still teach in the classroom *well* from time to time' or should 'collaborate' with teachers in developing new approaches and materials. Teachers commented favourably both on the way in which some lecturers kept them in touch with curriculum developments and on the fact that their students frequently brought fresh ideas into the schools. For their part, 'practising teachers' selected to work with students should be those who can 'step back from the chalk face and reflect'. The reciprocal share taken by experienced teachers in training institutions could be extended. One suggested 'a three-year second-ment – fifty per cent in school, fifty per cent in university/college'. The other side of this coin is that training institutions should be entitled to more say in the induction process: 'a probationary experience that is planned by school, LEA and training institution'.

The tension between such different views of the relationship between schools and colleges, teachers and tutors, is revealed in suggestions about the taught element in training courses. There is the same division between those who emphasize the dominant importance of 'practical skills' and those who recommend courses that 'balance theory and practice'. This divide is largely reflected in teachers' perceptions of major omissions from their own training courses. Among the five most frequently mentioned topics, those who advocate an emphasis on practical skills tend to feel that they were ill-prepared in classroom management and control or in working across the whole ability range, while the others pick out more apparently 'theoretical' omissions like understanding children's development in English or aiding their language development.

Those teachers who emphasize practical concerns write frequently about the importance of providing 'ideas' for trainees: 'ideas for English teaching', 'lots of ideas and suggestions'. Their own choice of language suggests a strenuous period during which students will be 'armed' for the classroom, bombarded with 'practical suggestions', subjected to 'total immersion', given 'more exposure to resources', being '*saturated* in children's literature/types of poetry likely to appeal (students/probationers flounder in providing suitable material – I did)'. It is understandable that vulnerable teachers who are still 'floundering' should value this element in their training. It is easy to suggest to them that success requires an inexhaustible supply of 'ideas' for lessons that will 'work' (almost regardless of the class and the teacher), of texts that will 'appeal' and of control techniques proved efficient by others. A respondent only in her second year of teaching articulates this viewpoint:

> I don't think theory is useful to trainees. A trainee needs practical advice/specific lesson plans. Theory only comes after practice. My favourite book is Barbara Murray's *English Lessons at a Moment's Notice*. Less useful are those books which merely tell you *how* to do things NOT WHAT.

The same young teacher writes about her own training course that it failed to prepare her for 'planning whole programmes of study for GCSE (I felt we did a lot of *brilliant* one-offs)'. There was no suggestion that programmes of study can only be constructed from one-offs if teachers understand what kind of learning they are to promote. Other respondents would have suggested that instead of the idea that 'theory only comes after practice', theory should underpin it throughout.

The division of opinion illustrated here can be defined in terms of Eric Hoyle's distinction between *restricted* and *extended* professionals. Restricted professionals are those who see their task as bounded by the classroom walls; they describe themselves as working at the sharp end or the chalk face and make a hard distinction between practice and theory. Extended professionals, without devaluing the work of the classroom, realize that it cannot be separated from wider ideological issues. Their work is influenced by their involvement in curriculum development, in school-based research, in student training and induction and in wider school roles.[3] In general, the more experienced teachers expressed views that could be defined as those of extended professionals. They see theory and practice in reciprocal terms, talking of 'matching', 'balancing', 'related' forms of 'interaction' between the two. Their view of training is of 'a combination of academic and practical', 'matching theory and practice'. They point to the importance of 'reflection' on experience. One respondent describes her vision of how teachers should be prepared in these terms:

1 Some way that develops their personal knowledge, experience, skills in the subject.
2 I like theory and think it's important when taught well in contexts close to practice.
3 Close, perceptive mentor-like help with learning on the job (the mentor should be someone with a theoretical grip, too).

Several experienced teachers also stress the importance of using any training period to gain a wider understanding of children and their development: 'students should have as much time with young people as possible', 'they should be helped to define *in detail* what pupils need', 'seeing children at work throughout the age range'. A balancing need is to place students themselves in comparable learning situations: 'they should have direct hands-on experience of learning what is to be taught', 'by practising what they will be making children do' (and this, of course, is also advocated by all the lecturers writing in this volume).

By contrast with the 'immersion' model of training, a few respondents argue for courses which emphasize a wider view of English as part of a child's total experience of education, dismissed by others as 'educational theorizing' or 'generalities'. One young teacher conveys her sense of the urgency of this in her underlinings: '*All* teachers (not just of English) should be made aware on their PGCE courses that knowledge/teaching/learning are *not* value-free and that English teaching now reflects the dominant ideologies in the field of education as a whole'. Proposals to change teacher education are equally value-loaded and ideological, and we examine two of the most common here (neither of them gaining much support from our teachers).

Proposals to locate training in schools

'Teachers should be trained on the job, not in ivory towers'.[4] According to Rhodes Boyson, whose article bore this headline, 'what we need are specially selected teaching schools – like teaching hospitals – where all the teaching is carried out by school teachers' so that 'student teachers can then observe the most skilled members of their profession at work' in 'the flagships of the profession'.

Such views are echoed, to some extent, by one in ten of the respondents to our survey. It is intriguing, though, that only two of those are actually secondary English teachers (and one of these, while talking of students working alongside teachers, refers elsewhere to the desirability of a PGCE course at a certain university). The idea that training should be wholly located in schools gets its chief support from advisers, advisory teachers, inspectors, deputy heads, and heads of year. It may also be relevant that only three had themselves taken a postgraduate certificate in education. As recorded in Chapter 2, those who had taken a Cert.Ed. (the majority in this small group) were the most likely to give a low rating to their training.

The desire to remove training from institutions of higher education is related to the feelings of a few (described in the previous section) that the emphasis should be firmly on what they see as practice (as opposed to theory) and that the present arrangements for school experience in training courses are inadequate. The weakness of the first of these arguments has already been explored. Teaching cannot be reduced to a package of routines to be noted and imitated; the skills cannot be separated from the accompanying principles. The value of school experience is highly dependent on the extent to which prospective teachers have been prepared to learn from it, as the evaluations of PGCE students demonstrate. The second argument, that school experience in training courses is a minor element, somehow undervalued and dominated by the wishes or needs of the training institutions, is hardly borne out by the facts. Legislation already requires almost half of the training year to be spent on school experience (a minimum of 15 weeks out of 36, and many courses exceed the minimum). There is no balancing legal obligation on schools to accept students or to meet particular criteria in caring for them, and it is not always easy to find schools where potential English teachers will be adequately supported. Although performance in the classroom is the crucial element in a student's assessment, pressures on schools seem to be persuading some that their training role is an optional extra. It is unsurprising, then, that in such times hardly any of our secondary teachers favoured wholly school-based training.

At the time of writing, the most controversial voice to call for training to be in teaching schools 'that would be like teaching hospitals' – that much repeated and very misleading simile – has been that of Professor David Hargreaves, head of the Cambridge University Department of Education.[5] (We note in passing that the professional education of nurses is steadily being moved *out* of hospitals and into higher education.) Conceding generously that 'the complete abolition of teacher training would be risky', Professor Hargreaves finds the present situation unsatisfactory because there is a great 'divide' existing 'between the practitioners (the schoolteachers) and the educators (the lecturers)'. His answer is to abolish both the BEd. and the PGCE (without suggesting whether work in that nineteenth-century sounding 'teaching school' would result in any specific qualification to replace these). Although Hargreaves cites Mary Warnock in support, her idea that university educators should be 'wholly academic, devoted to research' and that teachers in school should take over method work would surely turn Hargreaves' divide into an unbridgeable chasm.[6]

There seems little point in abandoning the concept of partnership, of complementary roles, advocated by our more experienced teachers, in favour of expecting teachers to combine the duties of 'practitioners' and 'educators'. Although the Oxford 'internship' scheme, described in a following chapter, increases the amount of time spent in schools, the authors make plain that it is not an apprenticeship model and that it is not predicated on being school-based. Apart from the practical problems of finance (Hargreaves admits that 'the more school-based initial training becomes, the more it is going to cost'[7]), time, and location (some of which are discussed in the chapter by Anthony Adams), there are more profound reasons for being dubious about placing the whole responsibility for training on the schools.

There is an inevitable tension between the major role of schools in caring for pupils and the need to allow students to experiment and sometimes to fail. In 'teaching schools', with large numbers of students, some classes will be taught by students much more than teachers or parents would wish. Hargreaves and others fail to acknowledge that the qualities of an excellent classroom teacher of English are not necessarily those required by a trainer of students, and a teaching school would be unlikely to have excellent staff in every subject of the curriculum. There is little point in assuming that schools, where according to HMI a third of all teaching is less than satisfactory, are going to be better places to base the training of teachers than colleges and universities, especially in view of suggestions that much of the wastage from training results from discouragement experienced in schools.[8] There is a major irony in the fact that those theorists who are most critical of the supposed lack of competence of teachers are often those who wish to put the training of teachers in the hands of these same people.

It also has to be doubted whether over-stretched English teachers, even with additional resources, could be expected to undertake more of a share of training than they already attempt. One said, 'We've already reached saturation point', and to undertake more training would mean 'no time left to teach the kids'. Some of the practical problems have been outlined in a paper by Judith Atkinson.[9] One recent survey found that many teachers admitted giving little or no guidance or assistance to students on teaching practice. Asked what they would have missed in a wholly school-based course, the majority of students cited 'the support of highly professional, skilled tutors' because 'professional support is just not available from often over-worked teaching colleagues'.[10] As for the second phase of teacher preparation, the Inspectorate's 1988 survey[11] found that 'a substantial proportion' of new teachers were dissatisfied with the quality of induction and support that they received on entering their schools (only just over half, 55 per cent, were reasonably satisfied). Three-fifths had received no structured induction programme. Under half had the opportunity to work alongside other teachers or to visit other schools, and the majority had no reduction in their teaching load. According to HMI, half the schools had inappropriate expectations of newly-trained teachers. Until this phase of preparation is better handled, it would be unwise to add initial training to schools' responsibilities.

None of this encourages a wish to abandon the present balance between involvement in school (frequently in a variety of schools) and more detached consideration of practice and sharing of perceptions in college or university. The habits of reflection, analysis and questioning do not come about simply by observing and imitating one of those 'masters of the craft of teaching' about whom the Hillgate Group are so enthusiastic. A more rational course is surely to aim for what Atkinson calls 'stronger links ... between school tutors and the training institution', especially since the Sheffield/Stockholm enquiry has

reinforced the recommendations of other recent studies that the 'triadic' relationship between student, teacher and supervisor 'should be strengthened, not weak-
ened or even removed'.[12]

The licensed teacher free-for-all

The most radical proposal for change is simply to abandon any national scheme
for initial training and to permit schools to offer new recruits whatever kind of
assistance they wish, unhampered by the CATE criteria for evaluation. A
well-orchestrated Right-wing campaign in favour of such 'licensed teachers' has
been repeating the same threadbare arguments with virtually no supporting
evidence, as though shouting loudly and often will somehow take the place of
truth. The small group of authors who write under a variety of impressive titles
like The Social Affairs Unit or The Educational Research Centre have no real
wish to improve the system; simply to destroy it. For them, the requirement of a
qualification in teaching represents another form of restrictive practice imposed
on the 'free' market. In its place they wish to make the licensed teacher scheme
the main entry route, with each school making its own decisions about the training and salaries to be offered, and with 'no need for external approval or vali-
dation of the training'.[13] They have not been deterred either by the findings of
HMI that the pioneering schemes have 'turned out many poor teachers' and
caused 'a worrying number of withdrawals', or by the fact that this method may
be considerably more expensive than ordinary training.[14]

The unsupported allegation is that the requirement to train, rather than poor
salaries and working conditions, 'deters good graduates from entering the
profession'.[15] In fact, when maths and science graduates were exempted from the
need to train in 1973, there was no sign of any rush from good honours
graduates, and eventually only a small minority opted to enter the profession
by that route. The English graduates with whom we have talked almost
unanimously say that they would not dream of teaching without preliminary
training, that it would just not be possible to pick up what they needed to know
about methodology and management, about the National Curriculum and assessment, as they went along. In fact, what deters the well-qualified from entering
the profession is not the requirement for initial training but these assertions that
such preparation is unnecessary. Why should they seek a career that has no
specific professional component, that any competent people can pick up on the
job? Demeaning the understanding, abilities and skills of teaching is an odd way
to improve recruitment.

We are asked to believe that mature men and women, in particular, find training an insuperable barrier (although over a third of those entering PGCE courses
are already over the minimum 'licensee' age of 26). When it comes to those who
are supposed to be attracted by direct, unprepared access to the classroom, the
same unlikely stock figures recur in each of the different publications: 'married
women' like 'the literate wife of French extraction'/'the French spouse'; 'retired

people'/'the retired businessman'/the person 'having taken early retirement from business'; 'people skilled in some technical expertise'/'engineer with skills'/ 'mechanics' who have 'a lot of knowledge to impart'/'the knack of explaining his knowledge'/'the knack of explaining to children the tricks of their professions'.[16] The publications purport to come from different sources, but the similarities in language suggest that they are part of a unified, self-referring campaign.

In order to push the free-market dream-ticket of licensed teachers, the political Right writers attack a dummy target: a version of teacher-training that is virtually unrecognizable today, apparently referring back to the period before the 1974 enquiry mounted by the Universities Council for the Education of Teachers began the remodelling of courses that has continued to the present day. The criticisms are loud but vague. We are told that teacher training courses are 'felt to be inadequate', that 'much teacher training is unsatisfactory' and that 'a large vested interest has arisen in the form of a teacher-training establishment'.[17] The nearest we get to any evidence for this is in references to the HMI report, *The New Teacher in School*, 1988, laying stress on the fact that one in eight secondary teachers observed was felt to be inadequately prepared (rather than crediting the system with the other seven out of eight). We are left wondering whether observation of novice doctors or solicitors (or, indeed, experienced teachers in schools) would have found a higher proportion to be operating much more effectively. There is no mention of the fact that schools thought 95 per cent of the new entrants were adequately prepared for the job, or of the fact that young teachers were markedly better satisfied with their initial training than they were with the assistance they received from the schools they entered.

It is certainly true that few teachers beginning their careers would be confident enough to say that they felt *adequately* prepared (how could they be?). However, in view of the repeated suggestions that degree courses alone should provide adequate preparation for English teaching, it is worth comparing student reactions to teacher-training with those towards their English degrees. In a recent major survey, three-quarters of the English undergraduates had criticisms of their university courses and almost half were dissatisfied with the teaching they received there.[18] This is hardly a basis for claiming that future English teachers would find their degree courses an adequate preparation for their careers.

To give some support to their discontent with teacher preparation, the authors of these documents return repeatedly to three myths about teacher education which they sedulously foster. The power of their publicity is demonstrated by the fact that a government minister, Tim Eggar, unquestioningly echoes them, saying that in training there is 'too much theory and not enough practice, that the trainers have little or no classroom experience and peddle pet ideas, including some political bias'.[19]

*The myth that training courses indoctrinate students with pointless
or dangerous ideas*

There are vague but emotive claims that students emerge with 'their brains
stuffed with the dubious material now taught in so many teacher training
courses'.[20] In such institutions, we are assured, 'spurious and questionable
studies flourish', espousing an educational analysis that 'derives basically from
Neo-Marxist or New Left assumptions'.[21] Students are 'exposed to pretentious
pseudo-subjects, uncomprehended smatterings, or shameless propaganda' by
colleges that are accused of creating a 'Blue Peter curriculum' and of embodying
'an intolerant proto-totalitarian ideology'.[22] The extent to which this propaganda
is taking hold is revealed when Melanie Phillips can write in *The Guardian* that
'graduates of teacher training report a downgrading of the academic content of
such courses and a dismissal by tutors of language, art and culture as reactionary
and elitist'.[23] Just who are these anonymous tutors who see language as reactionary? What studies, precisely, are 'spurious' and in what respects? Where exactly
is a totalitarian ideology at work, except in the works quoted above?

The impression is given that courses consist largely of sociology or history at
an 'intellectually undemanding' level, whereas even the Secretary of State for
Education recognized that 'the academic content of teacher training is now more
rigorous, the professional content is much less theoretical, and much more
directly related to classroom practice'.[24] The lack of awareness of the real nature
of teacher education and the total absence of evidence or coherent argument are
breathtaking. There seems no understanding of the fact that courses for secondary English specialists are significantly different from those preparing teachers in
other subjects and for different age-ranges. Nor is there any recognition of the
fact that virtually all the contents of courses are now specified by the DES.
Typical of the muddled thinking is the way in which the Hillgate group manages
to argue that education is a field in which one cannot define 'what intellectual
distinction ... would really amount to', but can simultaneously assert, without
apparently knowing what the quality is, that there is no education department in
a British university which has it.[25] By contrast, Her Majesty's Inspectors say that
'the quality of research in university departments of education has won national
and international recognition and it enriches the teaching on initial training
courses'.[26]

The myth that teaching is best learned on the job

It is asserted that training is unnecessary because all that is required is adequate
knowledge of the subject; the rest comes by experience. There seems to be no
understanding of the fact that the possession of knowledge is not the same thing
as the ability to deploy and exploit it for a variety of individuals in teaching. The
Hillgate Group and others all seem to see teaching in simplistic terms of
imparting knowledge to willing recipients. The sole qualifications for teachers,
we are told, are 'necessary knowledge' and some (presumably innate) ability 'to

put that knowledge across to others'; 'Education is concerned with the transmission of knowledge, skills and culture'.[27] They write lyrically of those people
with 'real knowledge' who have 'the knack of explaining to children the tricks of
their professions',[28] as though that might equip them for the infinitely complex
business of teaching. Professor O'Hear gives the most cogent expression to this
view, continually opposing in a loaded way what he calls 'practical' and 'theoretical' knowledge. The necessary qualifications can be obtained without going near
a college or department of education: 'Having a qualification in one's subject and
actually teaching in a school are all that is relevant'.[29] Beneath the sentiments,
the thrust of O'Hear's argument is to downgrade teaching by making it appear a
craft rather than a profession, a trade without a supporting discipline.

It has long been appreciated that any claims of teaching to be a profession
must rest upon demonstrable expertise that goes beyond subject knowledge. In
an article on 'teaching as a profession' published in 1918, Frank Roscoe wrote:

> Unless it is agreed that the imparting of instruction demands special skill as
> distinct from knowledge of the subject-matter we shall be driven to accept the view
> that the teacher, as such, deserves no more consideration than any casual worker.
> No claim to rank as a profession can be maintained on behalf of teachers if it is
> held that their work may be undertaken with no more preparation than is involved
> in the study of the subject or subjects they purpose to teach.[30]

That, of course, is precisely why the licensed teacher argument is so attractive to
those who wish to down-grade teachers.

Unfortunately, O'Hear's 'transmission' view that a subject degree provides the
necessary knowledge ignores the fact that the content of most English degree
courses – though good for the development of the students – is largely irrelevant
for the younger classes of schools. Method courses have to provide both the
knowledge (about language development, children's literature, media studies,
practical approaches to drama, the writing process, and those other subjects
largely omitted in university) and the awareness of how to use that knowledge in
the secondary school. The really damaging notion is that teaching does not need
to be accompanied by continuous debate about principles. Nobody seriously
suggests that practising medicine or practising law is an activity somehow separate from theory, and in education also practice and principle are inseparable.

The myth that teacher-educators are themselves unsuccessful teachers

Sir Rhodes Boyson elegantly terms such lecturers 'levitating pseudo-intellectuals
immune from the heavy daily chores of teaching', people 'who have ceased to
practise – or in certain cases have never been in the profession'.[31] It should not
be necessary to mount a lengthy argument against this myth. We have contacted
a good number of English lecturers in departments of education, and none has
taught full-time for less than six years, and most have double that experience in
three or more different secondary schools. We are asked to assume that the

successful English teachers appointed (largely on the basis of that success) to work in teacher education suddenly cease to be effective when they work with students in their 20s rather than with those of secondary age. In fact, they are continuing to spend much of their time in schools, on their own or with students, and were doing so voluntarily long before CATE required that they should all spend the equivalent of one term in five years working in school. (It is ironic that Sir Rhodes spent so much of his own time in school as a head teacher – a figure that really could be called immune from the heavy demands of teaching.) By contrast, Andrew Wilkinson has cogently argued that the typical tutor 'is at once a scholar furthering knowledge and ... immediately in touch with classroom realities'. In English teaching, he goes on, 'the climate in which education operates is one to which university teachers have made the major contribution'.[32] As some antidote to the harmful myths about teacher education, Chapters 5 to 8 give some account of the kind of work in teacher education actually being practised today in four different institutions.

5 Innovation in initial teacher education: the case of the PGCE

ANTHONY ADAMS

In the academic year (1989–90) during which this chapter was first being drafted, the University Department of Education in Cambridge, where I work, was the centre of a controversy over the future of the Post Graduate Certificate of Education (PGCE) in initial teacher education. This started with a series of articles published in autumn 1989[1] by the recently appointed head of department, Professor David Hargreaves, in which he argued for the abolition of the BEd. degree, the winding down of the PGCE, and the basing of most preparation for teaching in the schools. Indeed, his preferred model appeared to be the introduction of 'teaching schools':

> Teaching schools could help.... If ITT and its resources (including many lecturers) were transferred to schools, then all the supervisors of student teachers would have enhanced opportunities for reflection and reading.... It is when teachers and schools willingly accept responsibility for being the senior partner, using higher education as a resource to their work (rather than the other way round), that the teaching profession comes to its maturity. A carefully planned transfer of student teachers into teaching schools may also be a way of avoiding the greatest disaster for the profession – the establishment of the ill-considered licensed teacher scheme as the standard route into teaching in order to cope with the politically embarrassing crisis in teacher recruitment and supply.[2]

As a colleague and I have already written a public reply[3] and as the issues have been briefly considered in Chapter 4, I do not want to rake over this old ground here. But I continue to be concerned about three current ideas which underlie the argument. They seem to me to be closely connected and they are matters to which I wish to address myself. These three basic ideas can be identified in three words which have crept into regular usage in much contemporary discussion of teacher preparation: 'training', 'school-based', and 'partnership'.

First, 'training'. In his writing, as in much public discussion of the preparation of entrants to the teaching profession, Hargreaves regularly uses the term Initial Teacher Training (ITT). We can oppose this term to that other well established set of initials, INSET, or In-Service Education for Teaching.

There is abroad at the present time an increasingly well-established notion that all the beginning teacher needs is 'training', not 'education'. Once this is admitted, it becomes more difficult to argue for a continuing role of the universities in teacher preparation and the pressure to move it into the schools becomes understandable. Yet, it is curious how things have gone full circle. When I, still a school teacher myself, first wrote on this subject[4] I was told firmly that the title of a proposed chapter on the theme must be titled: *On the education* (not *the training*) *of teachers* since teacher educators at that time saw their role as being much more than that of mere trainers. (It is worth noting that the name of the old 'training colleges' was changed to that of 'Colleges of Education' specifically to make this point and to reflect the broader nature of teaching needs and underlining the importance of personal qualities related to successful teaching. It is in the light of this that my later comments on assessment of courses in section 3 should be considered). In an earlier article I have described in some detail the nature of the PGCE course in English which I was then running at Cambridge.[5] I stressed there how much the year on which the students embarked was one in which they grew, not only as potential teachers, but also as people. The course was devised with this in mind and many of its ingredients (journal writing, group workshop activities, multi-media productions) were designed to encourage this. Above all, we sought to get the students to engage, by the end of the year, in careful reflection upon themselves and their own behaviour as teachers. We have continued to follow this principle and have developed some new techniques for the purpose which will be described later in the chapter (see p. 66).

Second, in the context of 'school-based' training, I wish to return to the topic of innovation and urge that it is the link between the training institutions (in this case a university) and the schools that often makes innovation in the schools themselves possible. This view of the role of the training institution has been condemned as 'somewhat arrogant' (Hargreaves, op.cit.) but I remain convinced that any other route will lead to an inevitable stagnation of what is happening in the schools. Indeed, the eager embrace of the notion of placing the major responsibility for teacher education ('training') in schools by those on the political Right, especially the Hillgate Group,[6] suggests that this is a not-altogether unacknowledged motivation. There is invariably a tension in teacher education between whether we are preparing students for schools as they are or schools as they should be;[7] for the schools of today or for the schools of tomorrow. With the speed of change in our society, the increasing importance of the European dimension, the introduction of the National Curriculum in England and Wales (the full implications of which for secondary schools are still only partly understood), I believe that the role of the training institution to remain firmly in the vanguard of change is paramount.[8] I shall also hope to show that its role in providing the conditions for the introduction of change is an indispensable one.

Third, 'partnership'. I maintain that there is a false duality in the currently fashionable notion of training being a 'partnership' between training institution and school. It is a notion that has been widely espoused on both the political Right and Left and much of its philosophy is enshrined in the edicts being issued by the Council for the Accreditation of Teacher Education (CATE). So far from raising standards it may be that the very notion of partnership leads to an imbalance in relationships that has the ultimate effect of depressing them. CATE came into being with commendable aims: the improvement of the quality of teacher training and, therefore, of the teaching in schools.[9] I believe that it can be shown actually to have had a depressing effect on standards where they were already high and to have led elsewhere to a dull, uniform mediocrity, perhaps not unlike the effects of the National Curriculum itself.

All three of these concepts are central to a discussion of teacher preparation across subjects and across age ranges. But the topic here is English teaching and I shall now discuss in some detail the contribution that the current Cambridge English PGCE course is making to the debate. To achieve this I turn to a series of concrete examples and move away for the time being from the theoretical basis of the argument.

The place of information technology

When I first wrote about the Cambridge PGCE course in English Methods[10] it was reasonably innovatory, certainly in comparison with what had preceded it. This was because, coming new into teacher education from school, I sought to apply to the process the best of the practice that had begun to establish itself in the schools in the 1960s, a much more student-centred, active learning environment. Many colleagues came into teacher education at about the same time with similar ideas. We even created a forum, ETUDE (a regular meeting of English Tutors in University Departments of Education), where these ideas could be discussed and developed. Just as the 1960s had been a major period of change in the practice of English teaching in schools,[11] so the 1970s marked a similar revolution in English methods work in the universities. It was, in a sense, a period of consolidation, bringing the schools and the universities into a much closer relationship in their understanding of good practice. The question now arises as to what is the way forward in the 1990s.

One of the growth areas at the present time, and for the future, is the role of Information Technology (IT) in schools. In no subject, perhaps, is the potential of IT more apparent than in that of English teaching. Apart from enhancing the performance of old tasks such as, for example, writing using a word processor, IT has opened up new and important language dimensions. One of the most significant of these is the growth of electronic mail, with the changes in communication style that are inherent in this. If the proposals for the National Curriculum in English are read carefully, it will be seen that IT involvement underlies proposal after proposal.[12] Yet the schools, for the most part, are ill-equipped and ill-prepared for this at present. It is here that the role of the teacher educator becomes paramount.

In Cambridge, both I and a number of colleagues have a particular research interest in IT and language. This is partly fortuitous: our lecturer in Information Technology in Education is himself an ex-head of English in a school,[13] who first came to work in the department as a lecturer in English methods. Because of this research interest we are well read in the field, we attend and address many conferences, we go out and observe the latest work in the field. We live, therefore, in a research climate that is favourable to the field of IT and English teaching and, although much of our work is now being matched elsewhere, we were certainly a pioneering department in this area. In other words, we were behaving in a manner traditional to the universities, that of research and development, pushing forward the frontiers of knowledge.

We have built upon this research interest so as to transfer it into part of the process of the education of our students. Every English student is, for example, expected to learn how to use a word processor and has a workshop session on this at the very start of the course. We still begin, as we were doing in 1980, with a session in which the lecturers read aloud to the students from works of children's literature[14]; it is now followed immediately by the session with the word processor. But there is an important distinction here. In 1990 our students, straight from their degree courses in English, are just as ill-prepared in such areas as children's fiction or multi-cultural literature as their predecessors were in 1980; but at least half will already come to the course in 1990 with at least a working knowledge of the new technologies. What they need to learn now is how to apply that knowledge to the situation of their teaching in schools.

That process of application is something that can, for the most part, only be done through the work of the UDE. The schools themselves cannot generally help for they, also for the most part, do not have the necessary skills or experience. Many of the heads of departments in the schools belong to the pre-IT generation, though a few will have begun to dabble with word processing, this in spite of a huge involvement in IT in INSET programmes over the past five years and in spite of the demands in this respect in the National Curriculum.

Last year, for example, we experimented with a programme in initial teacher education in the use of electronic mail. In terms of teacher education this was a programme both of curriculum development and curriculum renewal. On the renewal side we wanted to give the students more direct experience of learning how to respond to the written work of school students. We had tried having teacher tutors bring in unmarked exercise books straight from the classroom. All the students in their first term of the course, visiting a local school for one day a week, would have the opportunity of some response to pupil work. But, without the opportunity for a continuing dialogue between the student and the pupil, this seemed to lack something of reality. So we set up an electronic mail link between the department and a school some thirty-five miles away. The idea was, in its origin, a simple one. The students would be paired with the pupils; the pupils would write in school and send their work to the department by the electronic link. The students would then send their responses back to the school in the same way. These exchanges were planned to take place over a period of about three weeks during which a real working relationship could be established between student and pupil.

As a means of delivery electronic mail had several advantages. It was cheaper than ferrying the students over to the school on a regular basis; because it is characteristic of the medium that users can 'time shift' it was possible for the pupils to write in their English lessons and for the students to use their free time to send back their responses. Because all the exchanges could be held on file they were available for lecturers to inspect and to advise on at any time while the project was taking place.

Working in this way, we began to realize very quickly that things were happening that we had not anticipated. A planning discussion between the school teacher involved (himself an experienced electronic mail user), the lecturers and the students established the idea of the pupils writing 'in role': they, second year secondary, were to be aliens seeking to establish contact with 'intelligent life forms' on earth. The university students were to be the 'intelligent life forms'. This gave a purpose to the use of electronic mailing as the means of communication. What happened was that both the pupils and the students worked in pairs and both pairs stayed in role throughout the programme. Thus the students acted as writing tutors but primarily by means of prompting, asking the right questions, responding to the messages they received. (They were incidentally learning something about the processes involved in producing this kind of writing.)

Of course, in addition to providing a forum for writing and response, both pupils and students were learning certain technical skills, such as the use of word processing and electronic mailing. Because the output and motivation of the pupils within this totally mixed ability class were very variable, the students also learned something about the range of work that could be expected in any normal teaching situation.

Finally, after about three weeks of exchanges, we hired a coach to take the students to meet the pupils, with whom they had so far been corresponding entirely through aliases, face-to-face for the first time. The object here was to take the various electronic mailing exchanges and to produce an agreed edited version which could later be produced by the students as an exercise in desk top publishing (DTP). So the four writers (two pupils, two students) sat around a word processor and tried to flesh out a final version. One of the interesting aspects of this was that the word processing program in use in the school was not the one with which the students were familiar. This led to a situation of genuine reciprocal teaching and learning: the pupils were the 'experts' on the word processing program, the students the 'experts' on the more formal aspects of writing, such as spelling and punctuation. A lively workshop session resulted in which not just secretarial and presentational skills (Attainment Targets 4/5 in the National Curriculum) but the writing process (Attainment Target 3) and much talking and listening (Attainment Target 1) took place. Certainly the pattern of relationships within the classroom was very different from, and more productive than that of the conventional writing classroom.

So far, in this extended example, I have concentrated on the initial teacher education element. But the INSET element was equally important. Although the class teacher was an experienced user of electronic mail, his head of department was not. The school already had a modem[15] but it was not being used – the class teacher had only moved to the school that term. Indeed, the beginning of the programme was delayed because of the need to ensure that the modem worked (there were some initial technical difficulties) and the necessary subscription to an electronic mailing agency was paid. The pattern of approaching writing and responding to writing that we were developing with the students was also transferred to the practice in the classroom with the pupils. They, and their teachers, including the head of department, were building up their technical skills in word processing and the use of electronic mail at the same time as the students who were working with them. The changed relationship between teacher and taught that we noted when the two groups came face-to-face was also there in the relationships in the classroom.

What the programme had done, so far as the school was concerned, was to widen horizons, to show ways of working for which (without our intervention) there would have been neither time nor motivation. It was an example of in-service curriculum development in action.

In practice, retrospectively, the effect on the school may have been greater than that on the students. There were some teething troubles, as has already been mentioned, and this meant that there were fewer completed exchanges of writing than we had hoped for; the limitations of time meant that the DTP exercise never really got off the ground. We shall repeat the experiment next academic year and, building upon our experience, it will be more coherently developed and built more effectively into our total English teacher education programme. It also happens to fit with continuing research in the Department into the uses of electronic mailing in English teaching.[16]

If we now consider what has been described from the perspective of the discussion at the beginning of this chapter, the following points emerge:

1 It was much more than a matter of 'training': the students were learning about how to write and how to relate to unknown 13-year-olds as well as learning certain skills and techniques. They were developing as people as well as young teachers; they were developing knowledge and attitudes as well as skills. They were, in short, being educated as well as trained.
2 It was 'school-based' but it was also 'university-based'. It could never have taken place in the school alone for there was neither the expertise nor the

commitment there to make it happen. It was as much a piece of INSET as initial teacher education.

3 It did not really represent a 'partnership' for at least three elements were involved in roughly equal ways – the training institution, the school, and the students – four if we also include the pupils as a separate element. I return to the implications of this towards the end of the chapter.

This, then, provides a model for initial teacher education which links it with the research work in the university on the one hand and the developmental work of INSET on the other. It provides a model for continuity in the teacher education process where the university provides a central link.

There was, of course, also 'innovation'. Nothing like this had happened in the school before, though there are signs that it will again. At least two of the students took the idea into their teaching-practice schools with them and set up an electronic link between two of their classes. They have since put up a display of the resulting work for next year's students to see; they intend to set up a similar link between two of their classes in the schools to which they have been appointed even though this did not exist in either of the schools before. The programme that had started by an attempt to solve a long-standing problem of initial teacher education (how to give students more effective experience of responding to pupil writing) snow-balled into something far bigger than our originally planned intentions. On the academic side, apart from its use as an extended example in this chapter, it has already led to the writing of one article[17] and will find its place in a forthcoming book.[18] The 'research' element and the 'teaching' element become indistinguishable from each other as in all the best university teaching.

I have spent several pages detailing this example partly because it has not previously been written up in this country and partly because it provides a perfect paradigm of the relationship between school and university in the processes of teacher education. It also illustrates the central role of the PGCE in work of this kind.

Multi-cultural language awareness

A second example may be given of something that worked in a similar way though with very different content and, in a sense, the other way round. It provides a further illustration, however, of how INSET and initial teacher education can reinforce each other, while emphasizing the centrality of the training institution in the process.

One of the recommendations of the Kingman Inquiry,[19] which has received too little attention, relates to the value of bringing trainee teachers of English and of modern languages together for work in the field of language awareness. This links directly with the strand dealing with Knowledge About Language (KAL) in the English National Curriculum and figures also in the draft advice on the modern languages curriculum given in Harris.[20] With a colleague at

Cambridge, a German specialist, I have been exploring the possibilities of work in this area across our two subjects over the last few years. In addition, during the current academic year, I have been directing a University Funding Council (UFC) supported INSET project on multi-cultural education in the three areas, English, mathematics, and science. Looking back on my earlier writings on the development of the English methods work at Cambridge I am struck by how little more than lip service was paid there to the two related areas of multi-cultural education and English as a second language. Over the last five years this has been greatly modified and all the English students now have at least some experience of work with pupils whose mother tongue is other than English.

One of the features of the multi-cultural INSET project was the close working with schools, usually directly in the classroom, of the three lecturers concerned. In one of the schools with which I was connected we decided to set up a pilot project on language awareness for the first year which, it is hoped, will lead into a more developed course in subsequent years. This brought together in a series of planning meetings, and a subsequent day's teaching, the work of the English and modern languages departments in the school (itself something of an achievement); part of this involved teaching all the members of the first year an elementary lesson in reading and writing Bengali. I took part in this and taught a Bengali lesson alongside my school-teacher colleagues. This is not a field in which I can claim any particular expertise, either with the language or with the techniques of modern languages teaching. However I was helped by the internal staff workshops that we developed to prepare ourselves for this teaching and, above all, by the presence in the classroom of three excellent teaching assistants, 12-year-olds who were first-language Bengali users. Several things emerged from this. A major outcome was the greatly enhanced status that the three Bangladeshi pupils enjoyed as a result of the lesson. The native English users discovered that writing in what was to them an alien script was overwhelmingly demanding, even in terms of the motor reflexes involved.

It occurred to me as a result of my own experience with this experiment that a similar exercise would be useful for my PGCE students so, in the next academic year, the lesson in Bengali will be repeated for them and I shall borrow from the school a number of Bangladeshi pupils to help in the same way as they had done in school. It seems to me increasingly important for students in training for English teaching to become aware of how difficult it is to operate in an unfamiliar language when you are a secondary school pupil for whom English is not the mother tongue. So, next year, as well as including the Bengali lesson as part of our course on language awareness, we shall also try to ensure that all students spend some time during their weekly school attachment in the first term working in an English as a second language classroom. My own experience of such classrooms and the establishment of close working relations with a number of Section 11 teachers grew directly out of the INSET project that I have been describing.

So, in this case, it was working directly with teachers on an INSET programme that gave me new insights into the processes of language learning and helped me to establish new priorities for what I was going to undertake in the PGCE course. Again innovation, both in the school and the university, had resulted from the close working relationship that had been established between the two agents involved.

In my earlier writing about the Cambridge English PGCE course I now recognize that we had underestimated both the need for language education on the part of our students and the role to be played by the school in the process of initial teacher education. The INSET programmes with which I have been involved over the last two years have done something to remedy this.

Another UFC supported INSET programme has, for example, been concerned with the training of the school supervisors who work with our students on their long teaching practice in the second term of the course. The usefulness of this training has yet to be demonstrated but it has had a number of off-shoots which are already proving to have been of value. One of these has been the production, jointly between the department lecturers and the teachers concerned, of booklets providing guidelines for teaching practice supervision and for the use to be made of the one-day visits to schools by students in the first term of the course. It must be said that in the preparation of these booklets the students themselves were as important a voice as the lecturers and the school teachers. The booklets are, therefore, deliberately written in a manner addressed to the school and to the student at the same time. We intend them both to be aware of the inter-related nature of their roles in the processes of teacher education. The following extract shows the kind of experiences that we, with the schools, hope will become available to the students on their weekly visits:

1 Working over a period of weeks with a pair of pupils who are weak or reluctant readers. This would involve some diagnosis of the problem and the production of appropriate materials and teaching for the pupils concerned. This may be particularly appropriate after the half-term break.

2 Observing and participating as co-teacher in practical activities such as drama and project work. There is also much value in observing practical work in 'non-English' areas of the curriculum such as science and craft.

3 Responding to pupils' written work by helping with marking, perhaps looking at one-third of a class's work at a time. This will involve talking with the pupils about their work as well as making written responses.

4 Undertaking 'research' using the University's facilities, e.g. finding resources, books, computer programs and books for 'book boxes' which will enlarge and enrich the resources available in the school you are visiting. The value of this is that it will lead you to explore the resources available at the University Department within a clearly defined context. This should lead you to think about resources appropriate to particular ages and abilities of pupils.

5 Participating in role play, in particular taking adult roles, e.g. Probation officers

in relation to the pupils. Such activities may be of help in connection with GCSE oral work.

6 Learning about the special strengths of particular schools, for example, TVEI initiatives, Mode 3 GCSE work, Special Needs, Media Studies, Educational Technology, Drama. Each school can provide different experiences of these kinds which can make for useful discussion in the Department afterwards.

7 Gaining experience of, and helping with, forms of pupil profiling and evaluation. It will be worth exploring what schools are doing about such things as Records of Achievement and Personal and Social Education.

8 Participating in lessons which provide exemplars of good practice in the use of library and library periods. You should also find out what techniques are used to encourage children to become readers and sustain the reading habit.

9 Reading aloud to groups of pupils or whole classes. This could be done by several students working together and could include 'performance poetry' sessions.

Again, this precision of definition has moved a long way forward from the simple process of school placement which was our earlier model (when whatever happened was a matter of luck rather than judgement) and which left both ourselves, the students, and the schools dissatisfied. The processes of development in both initial and in-service teacher education have consistently reinforced each other and provided opportunities for innovation in both fields.

Assessment

In the context of the kind of work with students that has been described it may be appropriate to raise a few issues related to the process of assessment of PGCE courses. Some years ago I was a member of a small research group based at the University of Bristol which was looking at the demands made on PGCE students so far as writing was concerned. In those days Cambridge was the only department represented in the group which still had terminal examination. Since I had always opposed such an examination and argued in favour of course-work, on the analogy of GCSE in schools, I was surprised to discover how many of my colleagues found the demands of course-work, especially in those areas of the course not related to methods work, a mill-stone round their necks and those of their students. Certainly when we came to investigate the quantity of writing done in a variety of subjects in five very different PGCE courses we were astonished at the amount that was required.

Since then we have abandoned the examination and replaced it by a variety of pieces of written work and I have come to understand the point of view of my colleagues elsewhere. Last academic year the total quantity of written work we were requiring from PGCE students for assessment purposes alone was greater than that we were requiring from students undertaking Master's degrees. Moreover the kind of group work on which the methods work is based is regarded as suspect 'because it is difficult to moderate' and, consequently, I am reduced to inventing individual writing tasks known both to myself and the students to be totally irrelevant to their development as teachers, simply so that the examiners will have something to moderate. This seems to me, quite apart from anything else, to be sending the wrong signals to the students about the purposes of written work in school. But things are much worse than this. I cite the case of one of last year's students, one of the most intellectually able of the group. (For what it is worth he is in fact just completing a Cambridge Ph.D. in English.) He completed a very successful teaching practice in a well-known school in the East Midlands where he was appointed to a post on the staff. Throughout the course he showed himself to be a dedicated and hard-working student.

He failed the course. The major reason for this was his failure to perform adequately, in the opinion of the examiners, on two theoretical essays: one on sex education, the other on gender issues in education. The sex education essay was 'too short' and contained too many quotations; the gender essay, according to the internal examiner who had taught the course, did not cite the appropriate psychological authorities. I did in fact read the essays and, as an experienced examiner, would have had no hesitation in passing them. On the essay on gender issues in particular the student, in discussion with me, made a very effective defence of his work which was based upon post-structuralist reinterpretations of Freud, showed wide-ranging scholarship and drew, in particular, upon some of the recent work of such Cambridge post-structuralist critics as Stephen Heath. I suspect that, in this case, the internal examiner was unfamiliar with this material and that, because the answer had not been expressed in the expected terms, the essay was adjudged a failure. It appears to me a classic case of bad examining where the examiner had a pre-conceived notion of the answer that was expected and nothing else was acceptable. (It is only fair to add that half way through the following term he received a retrospective award of the PGCE after considerable pressure by myself and others. It was accepted by the examiners that there had been an unfortunate clerical error, which was certainly the case. The student nonetheless continued to feel aggrieved that this in no way addressed the substantive issue of the actual quality of his work even though he was relieved to receive the award.)

Again, I ask myself what lessons we are providing for prospective teachers by examining of this kind. So far from encouraging the innovation of which I have written earlier, processes such as this simply enable the more conserving forces within education.

Much current thinking in the area of assessment seems to be moving in the direction of profiling. In the Cambridge department in the coming academic year there is to be an experiment in profiling so that each student will finish the course with a 'Statement of Teaching Competence'. This is divided into two main areas: (i) Classroom skills, and (ii) The wider professional role. In the 'Classroom skills' area 15 separate competences are defined, each of which is to be evaluated on a four point scale as follows:

A = Outstanding for someone starting as a probationary teacher.
B = Competent for someone starting as a probationary teacher.

C = Adequate with need for development during time as a probationary teacher.

D = Inadequate basis for someone starting as a probationary teacher.

- = Insufficient information to make an assessment.

There seem to me several problems with such an approach. First, it is essentially reductionist in its suggestion that classroom teaching skills can be broken down into a number of discrete areas rather than a complexly orchestrated whole. Second, most of the 'skills' (the choice of the word is in itself significant) are by no means a single unity to be assessed by a single mark. Take the following as an example:

  v.   Employ a range of teaching methods appropriate for whole classes, groups and
        individuals   ☐

How does one deal here with the assessment of a student who can handle one style of teaching admirably but who is less competent, or more probably less comfortable, with another style?

Other 'skills' conceal within them values systems to which I, as a methods lecturer, or the student may not subscribe, for example:

Teach controversial subjects in a balanced way   ☐

The section on 'the wider professional role' raises even more difficult questions. One wonders, for example, how one is to give a single grade for the following, incorporating as it does a wide range of 'dimensions', 'themes' and 'skills':

  vii. Be able to incorporate into one's teaching as appropriate:

        cross-curricular dimensions (e.g. equal opportunities and multi-cultural
          education.)
        themes (e.g. environmental education, economic and industrial understanding
          and careers education and guidance.)
        skills (e.g. oracy, literacy, numeracy and problem solving.)   ☐

(It will be noted how much of the jargon here has uncritically taken over much of the language of both CATE and the National Curriculum.)

In any case how is one to imagine a lesson in which it was inappropriate to incorporate at least some of the skills listed here under 'oracy, literacy, numeracy and problem solving'?

Such inappropriate ways of assessing students totally ignore the human aspects of teaching. They belong to the time-and-motion study mentality of 'if it cannot be measured it does not exist'. Nowhere in the 'schedule' do inter-personal skills or such qualities as imagination and intelligence receive any attention. It is an arid approach destructive of all that really matters in education. It seeks, in the end, to develop not teachers but instructors and there is no wonder that it fits well into a field that has replaced education by training.

Conclusion

Throughout the concerns that have been described above there remains one constant feature, that is the close link established between the subject methods lecturer and the subject department in a particular school. This is one reason why the analogy of the 'teaching school' with the 'teaching hospital' breaks down. It will be rare for all departments in a school to be of equal worth: I can think of two schools with which I work where the English departments are outstanding and much of the rest of the teaching mediocre. To provide the proper climate for initial teacher education it seems clear that the models and inspiration provided by the school subject department are of paramount importance and that the choice of school, both for initial experience and teaching practice, must depend upon the professional knowledge and judgement of the subject methods lecturer. In the case of English, for example, my own concerns, some of which I have elaborated above, mean that I want to place a large proportion of my students in schools which provide experience of multi-cultural education, language awareness courses, mixed ability teaching and some teaching of English as a second language. My colleagues in other subjects, such as classics or physics, will have their own priorities which may be very different from my own concerns.

It is not enough, however, just to seek out and use good subject departments. The department used, especially for teaching practice, must be the right one for a particular student. The choice has to be based upon the professional knowledge and judgement of the subject lecturer of school and student alike. It follows, therefore, that subject lecturers must be free to develop mutually supportive relationships with those departments with which they work. Many of the schools I use for teaching practice are ones with which I have worked for a number of years. As well as placing students in them, I am likely to be involved with them in the kind of in-service work described above. They will frequently appoint my own students to teaching posts in their schools, not infrequently the very same student who has done teaching practice there. Although there may be an unpleasantly élitist note sounding here one has to say that, for the purposes of initial teacher education, we have sought to build up a cadre of schools that can be relied upon to work in ways that are sympathetic to the ways in which we work ourselves. They may best be described as 'lighthouse' departments where innovation has been experimented with and where success has been achieved.

By contrast the models of teacher education which rely on placing a large number of students in a few schools (the 'teaching school' proposal of David Hargreaves) or upon a process of 'on-the-job' learning (the 'apprenticeship' proposal of Lawlor and members of the Hillgate group) are merely recipes for conserving what is present practice. Instead we need to seek out and develop the best of present practice into what may become the common practice of the future.

I believe, therefore, that in the best that has evolved in PGCE courses we have the groundwork for much of the advancement of the best practice in the schools. But this is not to be based on a simplistic notion of 'partnership' between the training and the teaching institutions. I have to suggest, instead of a partnership, an essentially symbiotic relationship between the two. But there is also a third element of equal importance and represented by the trainee students themselves. Rather than the notion of partnership, which immediately raises questions of who is to be the dominant, or senior, partner, it is more helpful to think in terms of what colleagues in Sydney have identified as a triadic relationship, in which the triad is composed of institutional lecturer, school supervisor and the student, all working together in mutually supportive roles.[21] We have seen, in the examples that have been given above of such a system, that the student is not a passive recipient of received wisdom from a teacher mentor; he or she will also be an independent contributor to the teaching and learning process, being also a kind of mentor for the teacher in the school.

Many of the currently proposed reforms of teacher education ignore this and this does not only include the ill-thought out schemes of such people as Sheila Lawlor. The very criteria under which CATE operates its approval of courses of initial teacher education tend to lay down a notional minimum 'national curriculum' for teacher education. But they do not take account of the innovatory nature of much of the best work that is going on in the universities and which is sustained by PGCE courses at their best. The requirement, for example, that lecturers concerned with pedagogy should have 'recent and relevant experience' of teaching in schools in no way explores the quality of what is going on in the schools themselves. My own experience of so-called 'recent and relevant experience' suggests that it is largely a waste of time; in no way is it matched by the close and developing relationship established by working regularly with a group of school English departments over many years in such ways as those described here.

6 English in the Oxford Internship scheme

CHRIS DAVIES and PETER BENTON

Introduction

In describing the Oxford Internship scheme, we are describing our own particularity and making claims for what that might offer to others. We are not attempting to speak for any other programmes, and it would certainly be a mistake to hold up the Internship scheme as representative of all ITT courses which can be characterized as *school-based*, and which make use of terms such as 'mentor' or even 'intern'. Superficial similarities might conceal profound differences, and we need to begin this account by outlining first, what we see as problems endemic in traditional schemes of initial teacher training and second, the distinctive characteristics of the Oxford scheme, before going on to describe how our English programme both exemplifies and benefits from the special nature of Internship.

Donald McIntyre has identified certain key concerns about traditional ITT courses that may be briefly summarized thus[1]: (i) Student teachers are often marginalized in schools, appearing as short-term visitors without the status, authority or situational knowledge to be like 'real' teachers. (ii) Educational theory is widely seen as the somewhat irrelevant and decontextualized province of the training institution, and practice seen as the concern of the schools. (iii) This split between training institution and school has damaging effects, not the least of which is that conscious examination becomes a semi-conscious trial-and-error kind of learning. (iv) There is often little opportunity to try out in schools even the practical advice given in college or university. (v) There is little value attached to the observation of experienced teachers and little help is given to student teachers in critically examining the range of practice they observe in schools. (vi) The quality of supervising teachers' diagnostic assessment of student teachers' teaching and their discussion of it varies widely, and school visits from tutors are often seen primarily as occasions for the testing of student teachers' classroom competence. (vii) In these circumstances it is hardly surprising that student teachers often learn to meet the different criteria of school and university staff separately, with different performances for different audiences.

(viii) Whatever approaches to teaching are offered, whether in school or university, in the final analysis it is the student teachers' own individual agenda of concerns – which may not be closely related to the official agenda of a PGCE programme – that largely determines their learning, yet, on traditional courses, little attention is paid to such an individual agenda.

In what follows we hope it will become apparent how Internship seeks to address such issues, not least through a close partnership between university and school and through jointly planned and executed programmes of study. That said, it is important to state that our scheme is not primarily about being school-based – it does not provide an apprenticeship any more than it attempts to provide a solid grounding in educational theory before moving into the classroom. It values both practical realities and theoretical perspectives, without assigning priority to either. It is primarily about a working partnership between the different and equally important perspectives of school and university – the perspectives of practice and theory, classroom teachers and UDE tutors.

Such an emphasis has important implications for teacher training in general, and in particular offers rich scope for the training of English teachers. Our partnership aims to ensure that our students experience and explore differing perspectives on all issues to do with teaching. It aims, more than anything, to produce teachers who will habitually refer to and make use of widely ranging knowledge, understanding and experiences, in their future professional lives. This kind of partnership is not achieved lightly. It requires everyone involved in the scheme – school teachers, university tutors, PGCE students – to be open to and considerate of perspectives and concerns that are, on occasion, at odds with their own. It involves what can on occasions be a real effort of mutual respect, and the capacity to open up one's own point of view for critical examination. This partnership is not about flattering teachers in schools into doing the university's work – we are talking of a combined effort to make the distinctive kinds of knowledge and skill that the various members of our partnership possess all equally available for learning from and testing out by the students.

The Oxford Internship scheme first operated in 1987/88, after a number of years of planning and preparation in conjunction with the Oxfordshire LEA and its secondary schools, with many of which the Oxford UDE already had a lengthy and successful history of cooperation. A detailed account of the whole development can be found in *The Oxford Internship Scheme: Integration and Partnership in Initial Teacher Education*,[2] but it is worth giving the barest bones of its structure here, and some of the more crucial working practices involved in it, before focusing on how our English programme operates within that overall context.

We now work with roughly 20 schools at any one time, with some schools withdrawing for short periods in order to allow others into the scheme. Each school has between 8 and 12 interns – PGCE students – attached to it throughout most of the academic year. These interns come in pairs in each curriculum area, and operate their own mini-partnership. Each pair of interns is guided most closely, in school, by the mentor – the experienced member of the school subject department who has main responsibility for the school-based part of their training, at least with regard to classroom teaching, throughout the year. The pair of interns works with, and talks with, the mentor; that relationship is at the heart of things. The mentor also makes it possible for the interns to work with, get to know, and learn from other experienced members of the subject department, as gradually the interns extend their involvement with that department, and eventually become (all being well) professional and reliable colleagues.

The school-based opportunities that the mentor organizes for the interns enable them to move from early observation and discussion of the lessons of experienced teachers, and initial attempts at planning and teaching within a relatively protected classroom environment, to more mature observation of experienced teachers, the mastery of essential skills, and the development of the skills of self-evaluation, as they move towards a state of real professionalism. Mentors provide opportunities for interns to test out and examine, as critically as they wish, ideas and possibilities promulgated in university seminars, just as they make their own experience, practice and expertise available for critical consideration in the university seminars run by curriculum tutors.

It is those curriculum tutors – as far as English is concerned, the authors of this chapter – who have the overall responsibility for making the scheme work, and for coordinating the activities of interns, mentors and university tutors. The curriculum tutors work with the mentors from the outset, for all interviews for admission to the course are carried out jointly (the candidates having spent a day in a comprehensive school before attending for interview). Curriculum tutors work with mentors to develop an agreed programme, to ensure that it operates smoothly, that everyone involved knows what everyone else is trying to do at any one time, and that the most appropriate kinds of learning are happening as the course develops. This means thinking carefully about where different kinds of learning need to happen, and about ways of ensuring that interns have access to the most appropriate sources of knowledge at all times. Some perspectives, some kinds of thinking and exploration, work better in the university seminar, and some in the school classroom.

The interns pass through various stages during the year, and achieve success in two phases. Until February they have joint (J) weeks, beginning and ending the week at the university, and spending the middle of the week in schools. Then they have school (S) weeks, all five days each week in school until May. Finally they have evaluation (E) weeks, back at the university department for some time each week, and the rest of the time either in their own or in other schools, broadening their experience. Altogether, interns are working in schools for at least 23 weeks of their course. The first phase of success is achieved around about Easter-time, with the acknowledgement of classroom competence granted by mentors (backed up by curriculum tutors). Then, relatively safe in the knowledge that they are unlikely to fail the course, they embark on a period of self-evaluation, involving examination of their own concerns and classroom practice with the help of fellow interns, mentors and curriculum tutors.

The ultimate aim of all this is that interns leave the course capable, first of all, of coping effectively in the classroom, and – of equal importance – having developed 'a critical understanding of the curricular and pedagogical possibilities inherent in various approaches to teaching'. It is that last quotation, taken from the Briefing Papers for the course, which provides the basis for the specific characteristics of the Internship English programme.

Much has been left out of this very brief account, of course, including the whole of the extremely important General Programme (dealing with whole school and general educational issues), which is operated through a parallel school/university structure led by a professional tutor in each school and a general tutor from the UDE. This General Programme initiates certain issues which must be picked up by, and therefore influence the design of, the curriculum programmes, such as catering for individual differences and catering for the rights of different groups. As the integration of cross-curricular elements into the national subject curriculum extends in coming years, our own experience in this field will prove valuable to us: internship has aimed for such an integration from the start.

Neither the professional tutors nor the mentors are paid for their involvement but the LEA has supported their work by making 0.2 full time equivalent (f.t.e.) available for each pair of interns in each school. Typically, therefore, a school with five pairs of interns gains 0.5 f.t.e. This time is shared by mentors and the professional tutor to give each between 1.5 and 2 hours per week for working with the interns. To date, the LEA has recognized the value of the scheme in terms of its providing a catalyst within the schools for professional development, collective review of practice, improved pedagogy and intellectual curiosity.[3] Moreover, as Brighouse remarked, 'a second and invaluable bonus is the quality of recruits to secondary schools in Oxfordshire'.[4]

The Internship English programme can be distinguished in three major ways: by the underlying philosophical basis of its approach to English, by the kind of planning we undertake in the interests of partnership, and by the way the different members of that partnership try to carry out their different roles in the programme. In the next section, we will discuss the principles underlying these three major aspects of how Internship English works.

Principles of English within Internship

The philosophical basis

We seem to be suggesting an element of uniqueness for English within Internship which other English tutors in other UDEs might want to contest, and at this stage we must say, hurriedly, that much of our English programme probably resembles much of other ITT secondary English programmes. There are certain concerns which come round every year, and a steady stream of fresh ones which force us to reassess, or even abandon, our approach to familiar things. Each year we work out slightly different solutions to questions of how to prioritize, sequence and combine the different elements that might reasonably be expected to appear in an English PGCE programme: subject aims, content and pedagogy explored in the perspective of classrooms, the needs of pupils, social justice and the expectations of society. The PGCE year is short, and the amount of new learning fresh teachers need to embark on is phenomenal, and in planning the course we do our best to fit the various elements together in the most efficient, productive and coherent ways we can, so that the individual elements inform and illuminate each other the first time – the only time – around.

Partly searching continually for this perfect arrangement of elements, partly responding to the continual pressures of curriculum development, partly needing simply to do things a bit differently each year in order to keep fresh, and always learning from our mentors about aspects of the programme that do and do not work in *their* experience of the year, we never arrive at some illusory heaven of the perfect course plan. There *is* no single such thing as 'An Internship English Programme'.

We do have an approach, though. In the way we plan our English programme, we consistently and coherently adhere to certain ideas and principles which work firmly within the context of Internship, and which have been developed and evaluated over a four-year period under the comprehensive examination of a doctoral research project. We approach the wealth of possibilities and complexities bound up in English teaching by emphasizing the idea of diversity rather than consensus within the subject – the idea of *different versions* of the subject co-existing, often uneasily, in the thinking and practice of secondary English teachers. Our starting point with our interns is to get them thinking about the fact that there are no natural or correct answers to the questions 'What is secondary English for?', 'What should it be about?' Having thus undermined and dismayed them, we do set about assuring them that there *are* correct and proper ways of thinking about English teaching, of dealing with the problems and possibilities of being English teachers, and that it is our joint intention to help them learn and develop those.

Asking what English is for, and what it should be about, succeeds in two important respects: pointing interns back to their own history as English students, at school and in higher education, and forwards towards the choices and requirements that await them as secondary English teachers. First, there is the central task of ITT to lead recent graduates away from the essentially self-centred and academic concerns of the student towards the essentially other-centred and pedagogical concerns of the teacher. Secondly, and an obvious next aspect of the first, there is the task of making new teachers conscious of the concerns and thinking of practising English school teachers.

As we said earlier, the Internship scheme aims to help all students explore the widest possible variety of issues to do with teaching from a variety of perspectives, and according to diverse criteria. In the English subject area, the first thing that new teachers must grasp is that there are choices to be made, both about what pupils should learn, and about the best ways of getting them to learn those things. Some of those choices can be made according to criteria of practicality: will that work in the classroom, will this clearly convey the ideas I'm getting at? In addition, many such choices are made according to an individual teacher's subject ideology – the belief system which makes certain choices more desirable than others. There is in fact very little reasoned and researched knowledge about what works best in English, and about what is most useful to know: the majority of teaching decisions are made according to an impenetrable combination of experience, received common sense, and personal convictions.

We do not attempt to replace pre-conceptions, convictions and ideology with perfect reason. That really is asking too much. But we do aim to approach the bewildering and exciting range of classroom possibilities that occur in the secondary English field within a framework of awareness. We want our interns to explore pre-conceptions, convictions and ideologies – their own, and other people's. We want them to consider the different teaching implications of those, to try them out and to assess them. It is their responsibility to make decisions and choices on the basis of what is best for their future pupils and to employ every perspective possible in the achievement of such open-mindedness and objectivity about the job. So the principle, the underlying philosophical basis, is that obvious and taken-for-granted beliefs about what English should consist of and provide must be contested, explored and ultimately justified. This notion potentially pervades all elements, however mundane, of our annual programme. We rely on it to provide a strong framework for probing received values and certainties about the teaching of English, whether these come from teachers in schools, or from tutors at the UDE.

The different roles

The notion of different roles is at the heart of the Internship scheme. As curriculum tutors, it is our role (as teachers, in addition to the coordinating role) to lead sessions in the university through which 'curriculum development and materials are placed in their various contexts (e.g. historical, philosophical, psychological). Interns will be introduced to a range of perspectives on each key issue and encouraged to reflect upon and to evaluate such perspectives'.[5]

In contrast to this, the *mentor* is asked to 'contribute the experience of an established teacher and the perspectives rooted in that experience to the development of interns'.[6] This is to be done both through the opportunities provided for interns to observe and teach (both collaboratively and individually) that the mentor organizes, and by the mentor discussing issues about teaching with the interns. Sometimes this can be a relatively formal, timetabled session involving interns and mentor sitting down and discussing questions about English teaching (in general, and in the particular conditions of that school), planning future lessons and reflecting on past lessons. Often it involves conversations in corridors, staff rooms and classrooms. Always it involves the actual and continuing experience of that mentor in that school at that time.

However wide and varied their own school teaching experience has previously been, the one thing university curriculum tutors cannot provide is that continuing, daily context of the pupil-filled classroom. There really is very little reason to try to do that, when there are so many currently practising English teachers ready and willing to provide it themselves. (And when there are so many other important issues and perspectives for curriculum tutors to be grappling with in university seminars.)

As far as our particular philosophical approach is concerned, such a division of roles is highly effective. It allows curriculum tutors in university seminars to explore past, current and potential English teaching practice and curriculum development in terms of *choice* – in terms of options available, and in terms of the beliefs about learning and teaching English which tend to determine any individual teacher's evaluation and selection of those options. It allows and encourages teachers to make their own particular convictions about the subject, their own classroom practice, and about the general reality of schools available for interns to examine. Thus, ultimately, the two perspectives of UDE and school, of theory and practice, can be mutually illuminating.

Planning the programme

It is in the planning of the scheme that we work out how the different roles within the partnership can best contribute to the achievement of all its aims, both practical and theoretical. The final version of the programme is put together by us, the curriculum tutors, in the weeks leading up to the arrival of the interns. Initial ideas have been explored during the previous summer term with individual mentors in schools, and in our last two full mentor group meetings in April and July. At this stage, we discuss the changes which mentors see as necessary to the existing programme. On the basis of these, and the other considerations listed in the previous section, such as curricular innovation, our own need for change, and the eternal search for perfection, we construct a detailed draft plan which we present to our mentors at a full group meeting in September. We ask them two sets of questions about this:

(a) Do you think this a coherent and logical way of working through the major issues of English teaching – especially in terms of current initiatives and developments? Does it look intelligible? interesting? enjoyable? possible?

(b) How do you want to work with these topics in school on Tuesdays and Wednesdays? In how much detail should we specify school-based activities arising from OUDES-based activities on Mondays? How rigid or flexible shall we make those connections? (As a rule, English teachers prefer flexible plans, but they need and require *our* plans to be rigorously detailed, and we are only now learning just how much detail is necessary.)

This kind of dialogue is hard to achieve, and we do not claim to have done that properly yet. We doubt if we ever shall, if only because mentors keep changing, and there is a constant process of establishing trust and mutual respect. So it does tend to happen that mentors prefer to approve our plans too readily, because they are still not convinced it is their business to comment on what we do in our sessions at OUDES. Whilst we are willing to do the work of planning and delivering the course, none of it will succeed unless the mentors are committed to and believe in that course to the extent that they want to follow up the same issues in schools – even if not from the same perspectives. Therefore we say to them, sincerely, that we do want them to carry an equal responsibility for, and interest in, the design of the English programme even if we, the curriculum tutors, do the work of planning it in detail.

The year of drafting this chapter, 1990, has been no exception. The mentors expressed warm approval for our draft programme, and wanted to alter nothing. This was either gratifying, or unsettling: sometimes it is hard to know what to think when people are basically being so polite and friendly. As far as the mentors were concerned – and they *were* quite straightforward about this, suggesting that they do feel able to comment when we suddenly get something right – the best aspect of the plans was undoubtedly the extent of the detail we provided in the finished programme this year: including far more precise information than before about what would actually happen in every session at OUDES. That, it transpired, had over the years been something of a mystery to the teachers in school: what goes on in PGCE seminars at the UDE? How do we spend the time? Naming the topics does not turn out to be enough – we do need to describe the sessions. (Ideally, mentors should be able to come along to at least one typical English curriculum day at the university department, just to experience it for themselves.) Knowing, at last, more or less exactly how we spend our time at OUDES, we can then agree on the kinds of opportunity that need to take place from week to week in school, and leave the specifying, arranging and delivery of that to the mentors, in negotiation with the interns (who carry the major responsibility for communicating their needs and expectations from week to week).

It is a delicate balance, and the successful achievement of a partnership programme, especially one in which one half of the partnership is voluntary, depends on willingness and not coercion. That willingness arises from a combination of understanding and enthusiasm – it is our job as curriculum tutors to develop a programme in which mentors enthusiastically believe, and which they are in a position to relate to what goes on in school. Such belief and understanding depends on far more than listing out the obvious and essential elements that any English teacher training programme will involve: it involves both probing below the obvious surface of those elements, and it involves thinking through what needs to go on in the teaching sessions that deliver those elements.

Thus we came up with the following model for presenting our plans *this* year: (a) broad headings; (b) the important questions raised by those headings; (c) details about the shape and different stages of each curriculum day. The broad headings are there to indicate the overall progression and coherence of the programme; the questions raised by each of those headings are there to open up the particular, unique concerns of that session; the details about sessions are there, mainly, for the mentors – so that they *really* know what goes on on Mondays – but also for the interns, who are adults and who do not need (does anyone?) to be kept in suspense about what they will be doing in a particular teaching room on a particular day.

For us, as tutors, such planning is difficult to achieve. Our experience as English teachers in schools, and sometimes subsequently as curriculum tutors, has taught us that, especially as that experience has increased, we can get by quite happily and successfully with just those major headings. We can fill in the details as we go along. But even if the sessions that emerge from that kind of experience-based spontaneity are adequate in themselves (and we doubt that, because there is simply too much to do in too little time on a PGCE course, for us to depend on inspiration and improvisation), such an approach makes a complete nonsense of the notion of partnership.

So the principle, as far as planning is concerned, is that we do it in as much detail as we possibly can, and that we communicate it to *everyone involved* (each other, the mentors, the interns) in as much detail as we possibly can.

The year in three stages – (1) J weeks
The greatest concentration of collaboratively planned new topics occurs in the first stage of the year – the joint (J) weeks (Mondays at the UDE, Tuesdays and Wednesdays in schools, and Thursdays and Fridays back at the UDE) which last from October until the end of January. In that time, within the overall approach outlined above, and changing from year to year for all the reasons outlined above, we attempt to cover the majority of concerns that any English PGCE programme would expect to cover. It is hard to list these things briefly, because each topic needs to be approached from more than one perspective. When, for instance, we look at *Knowledge about Language*, we also take the opportunity to focus both on lesson planning, and the giving of explanations. When we look at *Writing about Yourself*, we are also – and crucially – looking at the idea of *writing as process* as well as re-emphasizing previously encountered ideas about oracy, collaborative working *and* different possible ways of managing classes to encourage successful small group work. There is never enough time, of course, and every element of the planned course must carry such a multiple load.

The sequence of main topics in the J weeks period from October to the end of January involves, first, three successive Mondays devoted to establishing our approach to thinking and learning about English teaching. In the first week, we concentrate on the new interns' own past experience of the subject, and on some of the language used by secondary teachers to describe their aims for the subject. We attempt to make the idea of English subject ideologies visible, and to hold traditional common sense notions up to scrutiny. It is a very difficult business to introduce such ideas without being so aggressive as to confuse and anger brand new interns, or so soft as to leave them with the notion that teaching English is simply about doing whatever they feel like. At the very least, we want to make it clear that there are real questions to be asked about English teaching, and that the job of learning to teach involves more than adapting existing practices to fit in with one's own, possibly whimsical or idiosyncratic, inclinations.

This is followed up in the second week by a day's brainstorming about all the *choices* available to English teachers, or all the choices that English teachers *need* to make: choices about lesson content, pedagogy and the kind of learning the pupils are offered. Again, we are trying to help the interns discover what we see as the most appropriate way of thinking about English teaching, which can be characterized here most simply as: (a) as a teacher you have a responsibility to consider the full range of options available to you when you plan and teach a lesson; (b) it is not enough either to choose just what *you* feel like, or what someone else says you must. In English teaching, there are always multiple possibilities, and multiple points of reference to consider in selecting those.

One effect of that second major session is to open up the real and exciting range of options available to English teachers. The third week, to a certain extent, immediately threatens to close that down by looking at the National Curriculum. Our aim here, apart from simply meeting an inescapable requirement, and providing them with essential knowledge, is to help them to grasp what kind of beast the National Curriculum actually is: a vast, unstructured checklist of possibilities that in reality is not so far removed from the sorts of things brainstormed in the previous week.

Then, on the basis of this introduction to the business of English teaching which has emphasized the potential richness of the subject, and the difficult choices that English teachers need to make out of that richness, we move on to look at specific topics which are most likely to be new to our interns. These are topics which belong to, and most vividly represent, the world of modern secondary English rather than the English that most interns themselves experienced in school or university. Over the next five weeks, we look at *oracy*, *Knowledge about Language*, *Information Technology*, *video and audio technology*, *storytelling and the performing of poetry*, *writing as process*, and the *media*. Each of these is explored in terms of content, pupils' learning, and pedagogy, and is also related to major concerns of our General Programme at the time, such as the *individual learning needs of pupils*, *educational aspects of social justice*, and *assessment*.

At the same time and in parallel (we are pushed for time), we devote a large proportion of our far shorter Friday morning curriculum sessions to aspects of reading in English: looking at and sharing a wide range of teenage fiction, exploring experienced English teachers' approach to the use of fiction in the classroom, planning ways of using fiction in the classroom.

The final five-week period of J weeks involves concentrated collaborative work between interns, in which they attempt to develop schemes of work around the major areas we have just introduced and explored for the first time. Hopefully, this period of time provides the interns with a large amount of realistically work-able ideas to take into the approaching period of full-time school placement and, equally importantly, allows them to consider the rush of new ideas, possibilities and requirements more calmly than before, and from a wider range of per-spectives. Starting with the planning of a three-lesson sequence focusing on short stories, the interns develop plans around *Knowledge about Language*, collaborative writing, media and a full-length fiction text. Each of these ideas, developed by small groups or pairs of interns, are subsequently evaluated by the full intern group in terms of criteria such as the different needs of individual pupils, social justice and the rights of different groups, classroom management options, resources and preparation needs, integration with other elements of the English curriculum, assessment and recording of pupil progress.

There are other things going on during this time, of course: other things at the UDE (the General Programme, and a variety of options), and other things in school. Mentors are not simply, or even mainly, picking up each of these issues the day after we have dealt with them at the UDE. Sometimes this happens (and it is always up to the interns to negotiate with the mentors exactly *how* this should happen), but mostly mentors help interns move through this particular programme in school according to the particular rhythm of their particular school. Certain topics are appropriate at different times in school from when they occur in the UDE. Other topics arise spontaneously in school for us to pick up in the UDE – our single most important principle is that we agree about the major elements to be covered, and do all we can to ensure that this happens in a way that respects individual circumstances.

The year in three stages – (2) S weeks
A lot of the work, a lot of the interns' *learning*, that has gone on during the J week time in school has been of a highly practical kind. Interns have been learn-ing how to talk to schoolchildren, and to school teachers; how to take their place in classrooms, and how experienced teachers move in and out of different class-room situations with such apparent ease; the kinds of thing that constitute the basic competence of school teachers. As they move into the second stage of the year – the extended period of full-time placement in their school which lasts from February through to mid-May – they are first of all concerned with extending and consolidating that basic competence. That is what is asked of them, in clear and explicit terms, and it is on the achievement of this competence that their mentors will be assessing them in the final weeks of the Easter term.

Our role during this period, as curriculum tutors, is to work with the interns and mentors in schools, contributing towards the achievement of that competence. We help interns plan their lessons, and work with them in the delivery of those plans. We discuss with mentors their assessment of the interns, and observe the interns at work in order to corroborate those assessments, when necessary. In addition, of course, we try to keep the topics and the ideas that arose during the J weeks alive in the consciousness of interns, even when oppressed from time to time by the weight of daily school difficulties. In reality (because what we have just described represents a somewhat idealized version of what happens – different cases create their own problems, and bits and pieces fall off the most carefully planned programme quite regularly), we aim to achieve one thing above all: we aim to go into schools to support the interns, and to help them perceive the way their work is developing from week to week – but it is a constant effort for such visits to be meaningful, because they are at best sporadic, and at worst artificial and misleading.

The success of such visits is entirely dependent on the mentor, and on the quality of our relationship with individual mentors. Where that relationship is truly cooperative, school visits are productive and enjoyable. The interns are receiving rich and productive support within the school and we, as curriculum tutors, are helped to understand the learning needs, the progress, or the problems, of the interns we have come to work with or observe. If the mentor is not fully committed to the role (which can sometimes happen, for perfectly respectable reasons), or if the curriculum tutors have failed to convince the mentors that, for all their theorizing, they are also capable of rolling up their sleeves, UDE tutor visits end up as being as much, or as little, use as they ever were. Increasingly, the scheme having run for nearly four years, the majority of visits reflect a real sense of partnership and cooperation (which, for us, really is very important, because we spend from late October right through until June making such visits).

At the end of this period, the major assessment of the year is made, in which mentors assess interns as having achieved competence as classroom teachers, in terms of a number of key abilities agreed by all involved in the partnership, and published in the course papers. If mentors do not feel an intern is ready, then everyone involved – mentor, intern, curriculum tutor – works hard with that individual to improve that area of the intern's work which is unsatisfactory. If it looks as though the intern is not going to break out of this impasse, then we have to start talking about leaving the course. It is fairly rare, but it does happen, although in general most problems are solved sooner or later. Having achieved approval, which mainly occurs in the fortnight before the Easter break, interns are then ready to advance to the final stage of the year: self-evaluation.

The year in three stages – (3) E weeks
This, in theory, is where everything comes together. Given that nothing in life ever *actually* comes together as intended, we will describe what is meant to go on, before mentioning some of the reasons why that does not always happen.

This is the stage in the year when interns move from being strongly supported learner teachers towards being increasingly autonomous and reflective professionals, although it is also a period in which some highly significant learning from the expertise and craft knowledge of experienced teachers ought also to occur. To these ends, all interns undertake a process of self-evaluation, culminating in the Self-Evaluation Assignment, one of the two major pieces of writing they must complete in order to pass the course.

The major elements of the self-evaluation process involve the identification by interns of some area of their teaching to which they wish to pay particular attention, in order to solve a problem they have been experiencing, or to develop a line of work to which they aspire but which, as yet, they have not managed to achieve. This can be something very specific, such as encouraging small group work, paying equal attention to girls and boys during lessons, or exploring possibilities in media work. In addition, in the case of English, we also want interns to explore their particular chosen focus in the context of their overall – and by now, we hope, articulated and justified – version of English.

To this end, interns are encouraged first to identify and elaborate the aspect of their work on which they want to focus. They organize observation of an experienced teacher's work which can illuminate, in some way, the particular aspect they have chosen, such observation to be followed always by quite formal and structured post-lesson discussions with the teacher they have observed. Then they move on to a period, lasting between two and four weeks usually, during which they carry out their planned programme of teaching relating to the particular focus they have selected, and they evaluate the effectiveness of this through the medium of *partnership supervision*. This, basically, involves using another person – fellow intern, mentor or other teacher, curriculum tutor – as a source of feedback on what went on in particular lessons. The intern sets the agenda for the observation, and the person observing attempts to take copious notes designed to help the intern subsequently reflect on what took place, and on what is revealed about their chosen focus.

Virtually the whole experience is written up in a 5,000-plus word assignment and, considering the other pressures on interns at this time, including an equally long dissertation on a topic relating to the General Programme, the quality of these pieces of writing is extraordinarily high, and frequently extremely educative for us. We are certainly left with strong evidence that our interns are genuinely learning habits of reflectiveness that will survive the approaching pressures of full-time professionalism.

This final period of the year takes place once again in the context of three days at the UDE and two days in school each week. We are dealing with new topics: 16–19 education and A-level teaching, for instance. Interns are also exploring diverse personal interests within the subject, as well as completing projects for their school department. As the year closes, their attention becomes directed towards the first year of teaching, and we attempt to develop limited schemes of work intended to assist interns in the oppressive first few weeks of working as probationary teachers. But none of these things occur with quite the intensity of the first J weeks stage of the year – interns are constantly disappearing for job interviews, visiting other schools and trying to complete assignments. In addition, successful as the self-evaluation phase is, the university/school link begins to lose some of its meaning upon its completion. This is something we are now in the process of redesigning, although we suspect that most PGCE courses encounter a certain loss of involvement in their final weeks.

Conclusions

We are confident that our English programme is consistent with the main aims and structures of the Internship scheme, and that we have developed a programme that is distinctive and unique. Subsequent contact with interns who have passed through this programme (including interviews conducted as part of research into the programme) indicates a lasting effect in terms of the habits of thinking and reflection on the task of English teaching, without any sign of undesirable ideological single-mindedness (on the contrary: ideological certainties seem to fade somewhat during the first year of teaching, at least). Conversations with these interns' new colleagues, especially with their heads of department, at the end of their probationary year indicated a shared characteristic of unusual thoughtfulness about the task of teaching English among these ex-interns. Thanks to the immense commitment of the teachers working in partnership with us, we have been able to plan and implement an English programme which emphasizes and establishes habits of thinking hard about the business of teaching, of learning from the expertise of practising teachers and of developing a responsible and confident autonomy in the classroom. Thanks to the enthusiasm, intelligence and good humour of the interns who have so far followed this programme, this has been an immensely enjoyable experience for us.

7 Promoting reflective teaching: a Scottish perspective

COLIN PEACOCK

In the Scottish context, the University of Stirling is unique in its role as a teacher-training institution. The education departments of other Scottish universities have important responsibilities in the fields of research, consultancy and the teaching of higher degree programmes, but since its foundation in 1968 Stirling has been additionally involved in the initial training of teachers. This responsibility, though, is confined to the secondary sector of education and to a limited number of teaching subjects. English (along with mathematics, the sciences, history and modern languages) has always been one of these subjects and the joint programme involving English and education is well established.

The programme of courses in education that is offered is also unusual in that it extends over the full undergraduate course and runs concurrently with studies in other subject areas. It leads both to the award of a degree and to a qualification to teach a specific subject, or subjects, in secondary schools. For example, a student completing the programme might graduate with BA Honours in English Studies and Education together with a professional qualification to teach (the Diploma in Education) accredited by the General Teaching Council for Scotland. Although both the university and the department are comparatively small (3,500 in all with a present total annual output of about 50 teachers), our students come from all parts of the United Kingdom and beyond, not from Scotland alone, and students normally return to their home countries or regions to begin their teaching careers.

In contrast, the most common route for Scottish students who wish to become a teacher of English in a secondary school is via a one-year postgraduate course in one of the Scottish colleges of education. In this case students would apply for admission to such a course after completing (or as they approached the conclusion of) a first degree programme in which English Studies formed the main element. At the college students would follow a professionally oriented course with a variety of strands (including one directed towards the teaching of English) and probably three or four periods of school experience in a variety of schools. If students complete the course satisfactorily, they would then be permitted to register provisionally with the General Teaching Council and begin their career as a probationary teacher of English (in secondary schools only); the period of probation would be two years.

The experience offered at Stirling is quite different. Students would either have to make a decision to become a teacher before they came to the university and include education in their intended programme of courses, or, having been admitted to the university, they would take an initial course in education simply from interest, in response to the wide menu of courses offered by the university, and find that their interest and commitment grew. However, at this early stage in their progress and development no formal selection procedures or screening process would take place beyond the normal academic ones; no attempt would be made to predict their suitability for a career in teaching or to assess their commitment to it.

Once at the university, students would find that each academic year is divided into two semesters rather than the traditional British pattern of three terms and that the degree programme is divided into two distinct parts (Part One lasting for three semesters; Part Two for a further three semesters for an Ordinary or General degree and five semesters for an Honours degree). In Part One students would be offered an introduction to a variety of subjects and would have to construct a programme which involved at least one major and one subsidiary subject. If a student were planning to become a teacher of English, then obviously English studies would be the major subject and education the subsidiary, but it would be possible to take an additional major or subsidiary course in, say, history or film and media studies, as well as to complete further individual (minor) courses in other subjects, for example, philosophy, sociology, or French. There are no restrictions which limit students to subjects within a particular discipline or faculty.

If a student decides to continue with education in Part Two and train to be a teacher, he or she would need to take an additional semester's course at the conclusion of the programme which is devoted to education alone and is mainly school-based. However, up to this final point, the education programme is a concurrent one. That is, a student would be working his or her way through the education courses at the same time as completing his or her studies in English and possibly another main subject. In Scotland the study of a particular subject over a period of four semesters (or two years) at first degree level is the minimum acceptable to qualify to teach that subject in a secondary school; there are no teachers of English in Scotland who do not possess this minimum qualification.

Becoming a teacher of English

Traditionally Scottish students enter higher education after a broadly-based course of four or five school subjects taken at Higher grade (the 'Highers' examinations). Although this course is normally completed by the age of 17 rather than 18, more young people in Scotland are now staying on for an extra year at school either to take additional Highers or to follow the more demanding courses (Sixth Year Studies) which are intended to prepare students for the responsibilities of less supervised work in higher education. However, because of the long-established Scottish educational tradition which emphasizes breadth of study rather than depth, a first-year programme in a Scottish university is likely to be broader and more flexible than at universities elsewhere in Britain.

At Stirling in Part One of the degree programme students would have to complete eight courses (in three semesters). If a student were to choose English as his or her major subject, he or she would take one introductory English course each semester, the first directed towards the novel, the second drama, and the third poetry. Texts studied would be mainly works from the twentieth century by writers from all over the English-speaking world with some additional texts possibly in translation. Teaching would be by means of traditional lectures and small-group discussion. The student would normally be required to read at least one text each week but the demands would obviously depend on the length and difficulty of the texts being studied.

There are also two introductory courses in education. These are not teacher-training courses. They offer an introduction to the study of education from a variety of perspectives (philosophical, psychological, sociological) and are aimed at a wide undergraduate audience. Many students who take one or both courses do so out of interest and either have no intention of becoming teachers or plan eventually to become teachers in primary schools or in professions related to education. Neither of the two courses involves practical work; one directs students' attention to the nature of the curriculum in schools and current important issues in education, the other to the classroom, the teacher's role, and relationships between teachers and pupils. Exemplification is derived both from the Scottish educational system and from elsewhere in the United Kingdom (and beyond).

If, when students progress to Part Two of their degree programme, they decide to continue with English studies and education (for example at Honours level), there would be three further 'core' English courses they would have to complete (in semesters 4, 5 and 6). These provide a further introductory overview – the first on the poetic tradition (from Chaucer to the twentieth century), the second on Shakespeare and Renaissance drama, and the third on the nineteenth-century English novel. In addition, though, students would be able to select one or more extra English courses each semester from a wide range of options. These courses could be linguistic rather than literary in focus ('Discourse Study' for example), or, if literary, they could be either in-depth studies of a particular author (Milton or D.H. Lawrence, for instance), or, they might be thematic in approach (contemporary Australian or Caribbean literature, for example, or 'Feminism in the early English novel'). At the conclusion of the Honours course (in semester 8) students would have to complete an individual investigation. Here they explore the work of a particular author, topic or theme and write an extended supervised dissertation. Throughout the programme there would be opportunities to study works by Scottish authors.

The education courses in Part Two which run concurrently with this English studies programme are more subject-specific and vocational in purpose than the courses offered in Part One. It is in Part Two that students begin to develop their understanding, skills and confidence as beginning teachers of English. The Part One courses have provided an introduction and a context for further progress; they have encouraged students to reflect on broad educational issues and have made them more aware both of their complexity and often their intractability. Now, as students progress through the courses in Part Two, they begin the business of learning how to be a teacher. In this extended process, students are encouraged to reflect on their aims in teaching the subject; they prepare lessons and longer units of classroom work which can be tested out in different contexts; they learn essential classroom skills in the use of different modes of teaching and in management and control; and they learn how to assess pupils' progress and evaluate success. If all goes well, at the conclusion of the programme students should feel that they are beginning to develop into confident, competent beginning teachers with a varied repertoire of classroom skills and sound subject-specific knowledge. In addition, though, it is hoped that students will emerge as reflective and self-critical teachers, able to recognize and account for the strengths and weaknesses of particular lessons and the strategies they adopt.

In more detail, then, in the winter vacation before Part Two begins, students have to complete an introductory period of school observation and experience. This 'school practice' is normally based in the English department of a second-ary school near their home, with two weeks spent observing a range of classes and teachers and with a number of specified tasks to be completed. A further week is normally spent with a senior class in a 'feeder' primary school. In the course of these three weeks students will also be required to plan, teach and evaluate at least one lesson. Most students, however, take on much more than this: they work with individual children and groups, as well as making some more ambitious attempts at different kinds of whole-class teaching. This intro-ductory period of school experience is intended to increase students' awareness of the demands of school life as seen from the teacher's perspective and also to provide a context which will help them to understand the courses that will follow. Additionally they are encouraged (especially by means of the set tasks) to make connecting links between the content of the courses taken in Part One and the 'reality' found in classrooms and schools.

When students return to the university at the start of Part Two, the courses in semesters 4 and 5 are directed towards the business of learning how to be a teacher of English. There are seminars, workshops and assignments which deal with such themes as a student's varied aims in teaching the subject, different modes of teaching and classroom organization, resources, and assessment procedures. There are also seminars of a more theoretical nature which explore issues like aspects of children's learning, notions of ability, teachers' perceptions of their pupils and expectation effects. Central to both courses, though, is the practical dimension of micro-teaching which has been a feature of the Stirling education programme since its inception. The reading and discussion that students engage in, as well as the simulated activities of some of the workshops, are directed towards and illuminated by this practical experience. Pupils are bussed into the University from local schools and students work in pairs to plan, teach and evaluate small-scale lessons (lasting for up to thirty minutes) with small groups of children (starting with about six in number and increasing eventually to about fifteen). Lessons are video-recorded and students normally watch the playback of the tape immediately after it has been recorded to discuss and analyse the lesson and their performance in it. As the work of the two semesters develops, the demands of micro-teaching in terms of class management and extended planning increase.

In the winter vacation following semester 5, students proceed to their first major experience of classroom teaching in a secondary school (normally in the Scottish Central Region). During this period of 'teaching practice', students plan and teach lessons with junior classes (normally years 1–3) and observe the work of more experienced teachers with older and perhaps more difficult classes. Students are supervised by a visiting tutor from the University, but also (and more importantly) by a senior member of the school department who will work with students and discuss their progress. The purpose of assessment during this period of school experience is diagnostic – to help students identify what their present strengths are as future teachers of English, and to identify problems and areas of weakness for further work and development. It is at this point on the course that selection procedures begin to be applied, if they are necessary. Often students decide for themselves that they are not intended for a career in teaching and self-selection is an important aspect of the course. Occasionally, though, students are required to complete an additional period of school practice or fail to reach an acceptable standard. There are no academic problems associated with such decisions; the courses taken in education count towards the student's overall degree programme and he or she can graduate in the normal way (but obviously without the qualification to teach).

When students return to the university for semester 6, there are two major strands to the education course. For one of these strands they join students from other disciplines to consider the organization of the school and the education system as a whole; for the other strand they remain in their subject group to follow up in workshops and discussions any general problems identified on teaching practice (classroom management and control, for instance) and to consider recent developments in their subject fields – for example, the requirements of courses at Standard grade in Scotland and revised courses in English at Higher grade, and short modular courses in communication for older 'less academic' pupils.

If a student has been selected for the Honours track in English studies (semesters 7 and 8), an additional opportunity is offered in education – to follow a parallel track which will enable him or her to gain a separate Honours degree classification. To achieve this, he or she would have to complete an introductory course (taken by students with a range of subject backgrounds) on research methods in education, and plan, implement and report on a small-scale supervised research study. The English students who complete this strand often focus their research on an aspect of English teaching and the project is usually school- or classroom-based. In recent years such investigations have included the assessment of imaginative writing, cooperative teaching between English and learning support (or remedial) teachers, and children's reading interests.

The final semester (whether students are taking an Ordinary or Honours degree programme) is devoted to Education alone and it is largely school-based. Students complete a period of ten weeks working in one school, teaching classes throughout the age and ability range and observing experienced teachers at work. During this period students build on the foundations of knowledge, understanding and experience they have already gained, and develop their confidence and expertise as a beginning teacher. As with the previous period of school experience, help and support are provided by a visiting University tutor and by teachers within the school who supervise and discuss students' progress. There are also two breaks in the ten-week period when students return to the University to discuss problems, share experiences and ideas and attend classes given by university tutors and practising experienced teachers. If a student's progress is satisfactory and he or she reaches acceptable standards judged on a variety of professional dimensions, then the student proceeds to the next stage of his or her career and registers (provisionally) with the General Teaching Council for Scotland.

The concurrent programme that has been described is not renowned for its simplicity of design, but it does seem to work well. It is popular with students and held in high professional regard in Scotland. Figure 7.1 presents an overview in diagram form of the complete programme of courses and helps to clarify its development and the different routes offered.

The thinking that underpins the course

The concurrent model of teacher education provides both advantages and disadvantages when compared with intensive one-year postgraduate training courses. The Stirling experience suggests that extended time is an important element in our success. Students are given the opportunity to reflect on issues, to come to terms with and revisit important concepts, and to develop and increase confidence and skills as a practitioner. They are also given more opportunities to test out in practice not only the ideas and strategies offered on the course, but also themselves as future teachers of English. Students can make up their minds whether or not teaching is a job which they find congenial and attractive (without in any way affecting their academic progress through the university). The

Figure 7.1 Programme of education courses: Stirling University

	Semester	
September	1	Three courses: none in education
February	2	Education 01A2 with two other courses. Curriculum: knowledge, ideology and education
September	3	01A3 with up to two other courses. Human relationships in the classroom
End of Part One		

First School Experience: January – 3 weeks

February	4	01A4 with two other courses.
		(a) The nature and goals of teaching
		(b) Planning lessons
		(c) Micro-teaching
September	5	01A5 with two other courses.
		(a) Planning, implementing and evaluating a unit of work
		(b) Micro-teaching

Second School Experience: January – 4 weeks

February	6	GENERAL/HONOURS
		01G6/H6 with up to two other courses.
		(a) The processes of schooling
		(b) Subject-related studies
		(c) Choice from options
September	7	01H7 Honours (with two other courses)
		No courses in education: Honours 'with Education' track
		Dissertation on an educational topic: Honours 'and Education' track
February	8	01H7 continues with English dissertation

Optional School Experience: Honours students, June – 4 weeks

September		General 7/Honours 9: Education only.
		School Experience: 10 weeks
		In-service support at the university: 3 separate weeks
Course concluded December		

course also provides them with a framework of ideas and experiences which makes increasing demands on them, whilst offering different kinds of support to help them meet these challenges both within the university and in school on teaching practice.

From the outset, the training course at Stirling has taken account of the knowledge that has been gained from the study of teaching, the conditions that teachers appear to have to cope with in their daily work, and the constraints under which they operate. In English teaching this perspective has been derived from classroom and school-based research carried out by members of the department[1] and by reference to more general studies of teachers and teaching from all over the world.[2]

Similarly it was accepted at an early stage in the evolution of the course (partly because of the awareness of this research) that it is impossible to demonstrate that there is a 'right' or a 'best' way to teach. Different modes of teaching in the classroom are appropriate to different contexts and purposes; each mode – traditional whole-class teaching, small-group discussion, problem-solving and inquiry approaches, simulation and role-play – has both strengths and weaknesses given the context in which teachers are working and their aims and purposes. Each mode, too, provides a different role for the teacher and demands different kinds of professional skills – for example, skills of self-presentation and communication, of management and social control.[3] It followed, then, that two principal aims for the course should be, first, to provide student teachers with an awareness of the strengths and weaknesses of these different modes of teaching, and, second, to equip them with the skills which enabled them to teach successfully using a variety of classroom approaches.

Practice itself or 'experiential learning' has also always held a place of central importance in the course. Obviously school experience must play a major part in the training process and this practical dimension is traditionally the strand of any training course that student teachers seem most to appreciate and enjoy. Within the last five years, like other institutions in the United Kingdom, Stirling has increased the amount of school experience that students gain in order to meet national guidelines; the final period of teaching practice is now ten weeks long instead of the original six. But, as earlier discussion showed, an additional practical dimension has always existed in the Stirling programme within the university itself with the inclusion of micro-teaching in semesters 4 and 5.

Micro-teaching at Stirling has undergone an interesting process of evolution. Initially the practice was founded upon the analysis of teaching behaviours derived from classroom research and the resulting classification of essential component teaching skills. If a teacher were to teach successfully, it was argued, he or she would have to demonstrate competence in specific generic classroom skills – in asking different kinds of questions, for example, in responding to pupils, in explaining clearly, and in 'varying the stimulus' as the lesson developed. Micro-teaching in its original form at Stirling enabled students to teach very short lessons (ten minutes) to small classes (about five pupils); in each lesson students were required to practise a single 'skill' (like asking questions); and after the lesson was over they were asked to study the videotaped replay, systematically analysing the number of questions asked and classifying their type. The following week they would re-teach the lesson (to another class) to improve on their performance.

This approach was not popular with English students.[4] They found it difficult to prepare lessons that lasted only ten minutes, to concentrate in their preparation and teaching on one skill only, and, above all, they were hostile to making a systematic analysis and coding of their teaching behaviour. Although there was much of value in the programme (and an experienced teacher could appreciate the value), for beginning teachers the process appeared arid and mechanistic. It needed to be radically revised, and, as a result of research based in the department[5] and discussions with experienced practising teachers,[6] the present model of problem-solving experiential learning has emerged.

Students now teach lessons that are thirty minutes long. They plan, teach, and evaluate 'whole' lessons using different modes of teaching. In semester 4, working in pairs, they teach weekly single lessons to different classes (of 5–8 pupils), but in semester 5 (which is more popular) they plan an extended unit of work and meet the same class of about 15 children for the whole programme. Micro-teaching is now presented to students as an attempt to solve problems of planning, classroom teaching and evaluation; to learn from experience, to reflect on the strengths and weaknesses demonstrated by the student teacher, and to account for any perceived elements of success or failure in a lesson. Analysis and self-evaluation are still encouraged and checklists of skills for different modes of teaching are provided,[7] but the process is now seen as being less mechanistic than the previous model and more helpful to students' professional development. Micro-teaching is still not accepted by students as 'real teaching', but it seems to be welcomed as a positive and rewarding experience which helps in progress towards competence as a 'real teacher'.

The third dimension to exert an important formative influence on the Stirling programme of courses is collaboration with the teaching profession. In 1979, following the publication of the Sneddon Report in Scotland,[8] the University education department set up a joint project with the Central Regional Council to review the programme of professional courses at Stirling and to establish agreed procedures for the supervision and assessment of students in schools. The project was monitored and evaluated by a parallel project funded by the Scottish Education Department.[9] Subject-specific working parties were set up to review appropriate strands of the course and a steering committee was established to coordinate developments and review the course as a whole. The working parties consisted in the main of experienced, promoted teachers from schools, together with local authority advisers, and subject tutors and student representatives from the University; the steering committee included wider representation and was chaired by a local head teacher. The discussion and curriculum development that this collaboration encouraged influenced the content of the University courses and brought about changes in emphasis, content and sequence; it also ensured that teachers played a more explicit and important role in the supervision of students' progress in schools during periods of teaching practice and in their formative and summative assessment. A similar 'Professional Advisory Committee' now exists to continue the role of the original steering committee.

This process of collaboration was carried forward in a less public but perhaps more important way when teacher-tutors were appointed by the University in 1986. In the English field two principal teachers from local schools, working in different successive cycles of the programme, have shared the planning, teaching and evaluation of the courses in semesters 4 and 5, and have made additional contributions in other courses. One two-hour meeting of the class throughout semesters 4 and 5 has been cooperatively taught by the University and the teacher-tutor, using in the main a mixture of formal exposition, discussion and workshop approaches. This partnership has encouraged a developing relation-ship in the course between ideas, theory, and classroom practice, and teacher-tutors have presented videotaped examples of their own classroom work as well as case studies of pupils and a range of resource materials. In return, the partnership has created an opportunity for the university tutor to be active in the teacher-tutors' schools as a consultant, observer, and action-researcher.

Perhaps, in conclusion, the role of the General Teaching Council for Scotland should be emphasized as an important influence on the content and development of the Stirling professional programme. Members of the Council's Visitation Committee have regularly come to the department either to review the whole programme or to examine aspects of it. Accreditation depends on a successful outcome to these reviews and they involve discussion not only with University staff and students, but with teachers from local schools who participate in the programme in different ways.

Prospects for the future

The Stirling professional programme has successfully survived the changing demands and constraints placed on teacher education in Britain in the 1980s and we are confident about its strength and future role. Recent external reviews of the department's work by the Scottish Education Department (1987) and the General Teaching Council (1988) have been positive and encouraging. We aim to increase student numbers and teaching subjects offered in the coming decade as the demand for teachers increases. However, one of the acknowledged disadvantages of a concurrent programme, as compared with a postgraduate course or a school-based apprenticeship approach, is that it is much more difficult to use this route to create a quick and reliable source of beginning teachers.

In our own case, we first have to encourage students to come to the Univer-sity, their training may then last for up to five years, and then eventually, as they approach closer to the reality of a job in a school, they may decide that teaching offers fewer attractions than they had originally anticipated. Many readers (in the United Kingdom at least) will appreciate that in recent years it has become increasingly difficult to attract and retain young teachers, and often experienced, supervising teachers in schools offer the most vocal advice to students (and their own pupils) to look elsewhere for a more satisfying career. Consequently at Stirling, as elsewhere, an important source of recruitment in recent years has been (and will probably continue to be) mature students, especially but not exclusively women, who see teaching as a challenging and fulfilling job which offers them many opportunities. Perhaps, too, these mature entrants to teaching are less critical about its demands and the conditions of work it offers, when they compare it with the experience they gained in earlier employment or with the work of a spouse.

An increase in student numbers will also inevitably challenge some of the strengths of the programme we now take for granted. It will, for example, be more difficult to provide individual help and consultation to students, especially in relation to the practical work of the course. The demand for the economic use of staff time has already made the supervision of micro-teaching difficult. It can survive, though, in its present form without the investment of large amounts of tutorial contact time; once the procedures are established the students are capable of monitoring their own progress and evaluating their success. But tutorial involvement does convey a sense of concern and interest and it may be an important source of help and reassurance. And inevitably, any form of part-nership or collaborative work with practising teachers is also labour-intensive; it demands a great deal of time in discussion and preparation to achieve its results.

Although the framework of the programme offered at Stirling has remained in the main unchanged, the programme itself has been subjected to a process of continuous monitoring and development during the twenty years of its existence and it has shown itself to be capable of adaptation and change. At the time of writing, for example, a comprehensive internal review of course content is under way and major changes are being proposed. Important issues and concepts, like multi-cultural education, gender, and economic awareness in education, can be quickly and easily absorbed into the programme at appropriate points, when external professional, political or social pressures demand it. And both students and the teaching profession seem well satisfied with what we offer and have achieved. We have never been complacent about our success or our future, but we are now confident that there will be a continuing role for the department and the university in the production of a distinctive kind of beginning teacher – and not least in the preparation of teachers of English.

8 English in the formation of primary teachers

ERIC HADLEY

In this chapter, I want to consider the formation of primary teachers and the part that English and drama, in particular, have to play in that formation. I have chosen the word *formation* deliberately because from the beginning I want to assert the *person* at the centre of the educational process. That process, rightly understood, means that my students not only have *present* needs but they bring with them to the course a range of *past* experience and a teaching *future* beckons to them. In designing my courses I have to take account of the whole of that process.

I hope it will not seem perverse if I consider that teaching future in more detail and return to present needs in the light of it. Indeed, it has been the experience of working intensively with a small group of Mid-Glamorgan teachers over the last eighteen months which has made me re-examine the needs of my present four-year BEd. students. These teachers have been engaged in a Diploma course run jointly with the LEA and entitled *Language and Learning in the Primary Classroom*. Unlike the 'top-down' delivery model of conventional diploma/INSET courses I have got to know these teachers by working alongside them, talking at length about how they feel about what is going on inside their classrooms, responding to their writing in their journals and 'write-ups'. What concerns me most is how little, except in negative ways, their initial teacher training has impinged on their development as teachers. What struck me most was Lynne, an experienced teacher in her mid-30s, saying to me: 'College trained me to be one kind of teacher, my first head trained me to be his kind and my present head wants me to be her kind. I'm just beginning to realize that I could have opinions of my own, that I could be my own kind of teacher.' Breaking this pattern, the lack of self-esteem and the sense of powerlessness which goes with it, is painful precisely because it is so deep rooted. It is deep rooted and disguised by the adoption of models of what a 'good' teacher is, a process which begins at college and becomes deeply internalized as the years of teaching go by. So, revealingly, Lynne says of herself in her journal: 'Beginning to realize, more so than ever, that with all the demands on myself to be "Mrs

Perfect" in all curricular aspects I am not meeting the individual needs in my class to the degree I would like. I am spread too thin.'

Teaching then is conceived of as an endless series of 'demands', an agenda set up by someone else which you have to live up to – to be 'Mrs Perfect' – and which wears *you* out, wherever *you* are, that is, as you struggle to meet the demands of heads, LEA advisers, expert providers, NCC apparatchiks and ignorant politicians. The best way I can capture the state of mind of many of our teachers is to quote that voice which says in one of R.D. Laing's *Knots*:

> I feel you know what I am supposed to know
> but you can't tell me what it is
> because you don't know that I don't know what it is.
> You may know what I don't know, but not
>   that I don't know it
> and I can't tell you. So you will have to tell me
>   everything.[1]

What has been so disconcerting for our teachers is that we have refused to tell them 'everything' in order to explore with them what they know. What we agreed to do was, in Nancy Martin's phrase, 'be communicated with'[2] and give an authentic response to their classrooms, their talk and their writing. What this has promoted is a change in attitude to themselves as learners which has led to a change in attitude to their pupils. One measure of this is the change which has taken place in their language – they quickly stopped talking about 'linguistically deprived children' or 'language deficit models'. That is the way Mrs Perfect talks. Look at the way – this is early days – Lynne needs desperately to convince herself that she 'knows' and is in command of the learning in her classroom:

> My starting point is to see what 'styles' the children are already aware of, or have 'picked up'. This morning we thought I should leave my work as planned and see if I can identify what styles, if any.
>
> *Question 1:* How much input should there be from me so that I do not impose a 'style'?
>
> *Question 2:* Does the work I have planned provide enough opportunity for the children to show what they know?

Six months later she returns to the question of 'style' in relation to her pupils' journal keeping, itself a result of her own response journal. Having had her own views taken seriously, she now writes with a warmth that Mrs Perfect could not have managed:

> ... [the journals] ... became part of the move to look at a child's ability to find or adapt the 'style' they need to express what they have to say.... They express their views, almost as a test, expecting a reaction or judgement from myself. One now asks my opinion and sometimes replies to my comments. They write about their fears and find consolation in the fact they have someone to 'listen' and to help, if necessary or possible. It is also invaluable for finding out their views on classroom life and activities since they begin not to write what they think the teacher wants but what they want to write.

What Lynne has discovered along with our other teachers is, in Michael Armstrong's words, that 'Every significant educational moment is reconstructive, to however small an extent, adding to and altering life in ways which no educator can exactly foretell. This is why the best teachers have always been, often despite themselves, intellectuals of a kind.'[3] The last thing she, or the others, would have called themselves was 'intellectuals' but their ability to live with the pain of learning and the deep change in attitude and routine modes of thinking that implies, to be able to articulate that process for themselves and their pupils as a 'personal theory', seem to me 'intellectual'.

I have spent so long elaborating this view because I believe these are the kinds of 'intellectuals' I would like my BEd. students to be. This is why I began by talking about 'formation' instead of 'training' – formation at least implies that 'personal development' ('adding to and altering life') is intimately bound up with intellectual growth and the acquisition of skills. One of my concerns about the present climate in teacher education (including the CATE criteria) is that 'personal development' is a low priority. Lynne belongs to a generation of teachers who were 'trained' and in some respects the climate of teacher education has become even more narrowly 'practicist' than when she was at college. I have to assert even against my own colleagues that the agenda for students in higher education is *not* the National Curriculum. If we cannot learn on behalf of our students from the state of the profession now then Michael Armstrong is right, the effect of the educational changes we have been living through 'will be to stifle innovation, to inhibit the free play of ideas and to extinguish any lingering sense of excitement, originality and adventure about the business of teaching and learning'.

This is a point I shall return to but for the moment I want to explore further my hope for my own students to become 'intellectuals of a kind'. The potential students I meet at interview, clutching their A-level essays, for the most part do not see themselves as 'intellectuals' of any kind. Their ideas as to why they want to teach are rudimentary, though 'they've always wanted to teach' and 'they like children'. They are equally unclear as to the part their further studies in English and drama will play in either their personal or professional development, though 'they've always liked reading' and they're sure 'reading and writing ought to be enjoyable for young people'. Even if we had the time to pursue it they don't need a watered down university Eng. Lit. course of either the 'old fashioned' historico-lit. crit. variety or of the 'new fashioned' critical theory and women's studies variety. Nor do they want a revamped version of their A-level course.

Either of these options would be inappropriate for other reasons:

1 Most of my students when they enter our courses are not independent, voracious readers with an appetite for print and strongly developed personal tastes. They have become dutiful readers dominated by set-book approaches – line by line exegesis and lots of note-taking.
2 Many are not what I would call 'critical' readers able to explore the pre-

suppositions underlying a text and the non-explicit inferences which might be drawn from it. To put it simply their appreciation of irony is under-developed.

3 They often doubt and underestimate their own powers of expression as writers, in discussion and most of all as performers and readers (aloud) of a text, and again I would have to say that these inhibitions have often been confirmed by their sixth form and earlier experience of English.

On the other hand they have qualities as readers which suggest a different kind of potential:

1 'Innocent' readers they may be but they are thorough and the comparatively few things they have read stay with them and are possessed. They make me feel that my head is cluttered, that I read too much, too quickly.

2 Their reading may not be 'critical' but it is 'located' in personal experience, in the people they have shared books with, in the places and occasions they have been reading.

3 Their most refreshing quality is their lack of pretence. They may be 'untheorized' but they are not so intent on covering the precariousness of their real grasp on anything with fatuous glibness. They still dare to do things that undergraduates are too embarrassed to do, like ask what words mean or admit they don't understand. Nor are they in awe of the texts they encounter which enables them at times to feel and understand with an openness and directness I envy – like the student, herself the gentlest of people and, I know, a Christian, who said to me on the way out of a seminar on Donne's *Nocturnal upon St. Lucies Day* – 'He never once in that poem allows himself recourse to the consolation of Christianity.'

I have placed this emphasis on the kind of *readers* my students are when they arrive on the course because the kind of readers they become by the end of the course will affect the experience of reading for large numbers of primary age children for many years to come. It is a way of asserting too that although I do not wish the courses I am involved in to become narrowly 'practicist' the issue of English and trainee primary teachers has to be addressed in its intellectual, personal and professional dimensions throughout and across the whole BEd. course. This issue is not addressed simply by courses in 'curriculum leadership' or by separate development within the course of the 25 per cent of 'subject studies' time designated by the CATE criteria for specifically curriculum issues. It is also why I am glad that I was originally appointed to my present institution as a senior lecturer in English *and* professional studies. It must be immensely difficult to establish the unity of conception of a course and demonstrate what English and drama have to offer to a trainee primary teacher where this is not the case. I suppose we are lucky that a student's course is integrated to the extent that *their* teacher manifests that integration – by providing a personal model (that it is, for example, possible to teach *King Lear* in the morning and be reading stories to a reception class in the afternoon) that holds the apparently disparate 'reading worlds' of the course together, by moving with our students from lecture rooms to classrooms and back again as teachers, supervisors, facilitators and, I hope, learners.

It is much more difficult to legislate integration into a course where there are divisions between 'academic' staff, 'curriculum' staff, 'professional' staff, etc. My students need teachers with whom they can feel an identity of interest and a relationship and they would not feel the same way about 'English' and 'us' (as a section) if they did not know us as their teachers, workers *alongside* them in classrooms, teachers *independent* of them with our own interests in the primary classroom. As an English and drama section we have had to recently face the consequences of a major change in the organization and delivery of the BEd. course as a whole. Instead of subject studies courses running concurrently throughout the four years alongside education and teaching studies elements, courses are now delivered intermittently on a 'modular' basis – two 'modules' of English and drama in each year of the course. I would have to say that the shift to this new structure has brought some unsuspected advantages to subject studies. We have gained the possibility of a new intensity of working and flexibility in timing and approaches. When they are up and running our courses feel less diluted and all students have said that the new system makes them feel more like 'students'. They enjoy the sense of identity and course ownership which emerges from working with regularly constituted and smaller groups, tutors who know who they are and who demonstrate the thought and effort they have given to courses.

Problems arise because there is no adequate arrangement for contact with students in between modules. At the moment continuity of working styles, of reading and writing and informal contact has been sacrificed to a timetabling convenience which leads to frustration on the part of staff and students. I mention this to illustrate yet again that many of us are living through periods of institutional change where those responsible seem to display not the slightest subtlety or refinement about teaching and learning. As my expressive arts colleagues point out, 'practice' is essential to their discipline but what place is there in between modules for it to happen? As for our students – just to stay with *reading* for a moment – readers read at different rates, impressions and conceptions form and are developed over time, readers (particularly our readers) value support and opportunity to share ideas and experiences. We are in danger of teaching our students that there is no place for leisure in their courses and of confirming what BEd. courses, with what can be a bewildering and kaleidoscopic array of courses, personnel, changes of role, already confuse, namely the distinction between *intensity* (of thought, expression, endeavour) and *keeping busy* – all the more disastrous when that same confusion lies at the heart of so much poor primary practice.

Intensity is something which we try to make the characteristic of our first year English and drama course – if momentum is not built up quickly then students will slump back into that sixth form passivity so many of them are practised in. We begin our course working together in small groups, trying to get poems off the page, exploring their voices and our own and then coming together to share and present what we have discovered. It all sounds so simple, so obvious – so why do we meet so few students who have worked in this way before? On the other hand, in making it seem so simple, I am doing an injustice to the speed and range of discovery and adjustment that our students can make.

As I watched our first year students performing a group of poems for their expressive arts peers after two days of our programme this year I pondered on how far they had come and how many different hares we had set off. With the help of Edwin Morgan's *Message Clear*, we had learned how to read again and in company with our other authors, had discovered that the tone of a poem begins in finding and testing its voice(s); we had learned that it helps to have a few people around to do this testing; to argue, disagree, come to conclusions and that in the process all kinds of questions and answers about meanings and intentions arise. It was beginning to occur to people that reading aloud was perhaps the first act of criticism, that here thought and expression came together with courage – the courage to forget about self and concentrate on meaning and communication, that, again, collaboration and a sense of a specific audience help. We certainly learned that afternoon that an audience can affect a performer by, in Peter Brook's phrase, 'the quality of its attention.'[4]

As we moved from Miroslav Holub to Edwin Morgan, to Carl Sandburg, to Oswald Mtshali to John Agard, and I watched my students trying to locate those distinctive voices and I considered the demands it had made upon them, Czeslaw Milosz's words came into my mind:

> The purpose of poetry is to remind us
> how difficult it is to remain just one person,
> for our house is open, there are no keys in the doors
> and invisible guests come in and out at will[5]

words I shall want to come back to later. Just as there were other words in my mind as we finished the afternoon with John Agard's *Poetry Jump Up* – 'I is a poem today' – the words of the junior pupil who came up to me, after an afternoon of exploring poetry, including this one, with my year 3 students last year, and said – 'It was like a party'.

What my students have spent their time relearning or in many cases discovering for the first time is that such active encounters with texts can release the 'free play of ideas' and promote 'excitement, originality and adventure'. I think such encounters have to be central to the experience our course is offering throughout its length and not just at the beginning. I say this, as ever, with an eye to a future in school where our students as teachers can make such encounters occasions for celebration instead of the dreadful exhaustions of energy in pursuit of conspicuous display which characterizes, say, the 'celebration' of Christmas or, in this part of the world, St David's Day – anything less 'like a party' I cannot imagine.

This is another way of saying that, as they move forward to explore, question and find some shaping expression at their own adult level, there need to be occasions where they can reflect on their own experience in the light of their own developing knowledge of children and their needs. The emphasis on the reciprocity of learning which the teachers I described in my opening have had to painfully relearn needs to be asserted and maintained throughout initial training. The students have (re)discovered something about the nature of poetry – they have been engaged 'in a struggle for meaning', they will 'never forget the words', they understand the 'pleasure of conquering misunderstanding' and that 'every time you come to a new text it's like learning to read again'. They have felt the power of poetry in their own lives and have understood again what it is to 'learn without realizing that you're learning'. Now we have some reflections and considerations we can take into our thoughts about poetry and young people. With our first year students that means thinking about pre-school and infant children as that is the emphasis in that year of the course as a whole, though in saying that I want to make important distinctions between *our* emphasis and the emphasis of other aspects of the BEd. course.

We have not asked our students to be 'infantile' in either their behaviour or thought. If they have regained pleasure and confidence in their own learning – it is interesting how many, of the student comments state or imply a sense of mastery – then they are ready to consider the centrality of poetry and the part it plays in gaining mastery over the language and over the self for young children. As we move on to consider nursery rhymes and poetry for young children we are holding on to the notion too that *knowledge about language* has to be seen in the context of personal growth. Even more important is our determination to maintain the connection between the fully adult intelligence responding to 'adult' texts and that same intelligence responding to and mediating 'children's' texts.

This can meet with some resistance from the students themselves. As with their attitude to very young children, they do not mind being sentimental about them but think about them, make judgements, discriminate quality – that is a different matter. I had an argument with some students recently about Maurice Sendak's *In the Night Kitchen* and what became clear was that they did not know how to read it and because it did not yield up its meaning immediately in a conventional narrative they dismissed it. The fact that it is a marvellously outrageous poetic text, using language at full stretch and demanding that its readers meet that with their expressiveness at full stretch, had escaped them. Yet, to be fair, the moment they begin to test out the text with a view to reading, their views begin to modify. Part of the problem is that we have to overcome prejudice on the part of our students – they have to recognize that, for example, Maurice Sendak or Ruth Craft or Allan Ahlberg are 'real' writers who have chosen to write for children. They have to be convinced that they can bring their adult intelligence to bear on discriminating amongst the many texts which are available to children to distinguish those texts which in Margaret Meek's title 'teach what readers learn'.

In fact, I think an English and drama course for primary students has got to be raising that issue about *all* the texts they encounter. Indeed I would say that, particularly in our first year course, the questions we raise about texts for children and their mediation help to 'theorize' in a new way the *adult* reading our students are engaged in. Our thoughts about the nature of story, narrative forms, transmission, 'versions' of stories for children are often for our students the first time they ask questions about the dominant story forms – short stories and novels – in their experience. We try, not always successfully, to choose texts which sophisticate that reflection about themselves as readers, by introducing them to 'new' texts which we are all learning to read like John Berger's *Pig Earth* or Nadine Gordimer's *July's People*; or by exploring how one text helps or disables us from reading another as with, say, *Jane Eyre* and *Wide Sargasso Sea*; or by learning to read an author as he or she finds 'their own voice' and develops it, as, for example, in the early Lawrence.

Gradually what I hope develops is a realization that, unlike the message they have brought from much of their own schooling, encounters with texts are not exercises for some future engagement – that extraordinary solo communication to a silent unresponding audience called 'the exam'. Our interests are changing and developing but they are immediate, for ourselves and for the children we will help to make readers.

I hope that what is beginning to emerge is that our English and drama course does have a concern for the 3Rs – Remediation, Reflection and Resistance. I think I have probably said enough about the first item in terms of the nature of our students as readers to suggest some of the changes of attitude we need to encourage. The second is more problematic because, as with the teachers I began with, it means refusing to yield to the pressures to tell and it means exploring different ways of recording reflection. The only kind of recording most of our students are used to is the regular essay based on notes made in teaching sessions. We take this security away from our students, we demand difficult styles of working, a more collaborative, participatory approach, but we have been slow to develop alternative forms of reflection. With our teachers a response journal worked very well. It became the place where we entered into dialogue with someone else's ideas. We are experimenting with a modified version of this with our first year students as the place which might contain their individual 'literary and textual journey' throughout the year. The situation is further complicated by the fact that, on the one hand, I want them to rediscover the pleasure of learning inconspicuously (to use Frank Smith's phrase) both because it is the most powerful way we and children learn and because they have had conspicuous learning of a misguided variety until it is coming out of their ears. On the other hand they do need to be more conspicuously *conscious* and *theorized* than they are on behalf of their future pupils. I think that encouraging our students to talk and write collaboratively about what is at stake in their learning in a more sustained fashion on our part is likely to come nearer to that ideal I have of learners who think and talk with a pen in their hand.

And Resistance: it has always seemed to me that the stuff of English and drama is dangerous to pedagogy, the voices it introduces owe no allegiance to classrooms. If I read the words I quoted earlier from Czeslaw Milosz to my students and encourage them to explore their experience and texts in that spirit then we cannot help challenging the rigidity of personality and delight in routine which the narrow practicism of many of their other courses confirms. This is one antidote we can prescribe against Mrs Perfect and I can think of no one who challenges rigidity of personality quite like Chekhov. How much longer I can go on doing that when senior colleagues ask, 'What contribution is Chekhov making to the development of your students as curriculum leaders?' Here is my answer: last year my third year students and I spent a day working under the direction of an actress friend who has performed Chekhov (under a Russian director). Our text was *Three Sisters*. The day began with an exhausting physical and vocal workout. We spent the rest of the day working on the opening scenes, having our performance and interpretation challenged all the time by our director. The scrutiny we had to undergo was as rigorous as the workout; there was no going on until delivery and gesture had been subjected to trial and argument, until intention and motivation had been tested in performance. What confronted my students in that workshop was:

(a) Real expertise, rooted in regular practice and self-discipline, the polar opposite of 'non-specialism' foundering on muddled good intentions.
(b) Talent, which always confounds those who are committed to normative and linear modes of development.
(c) High critical expectation, which reserves its praise for those rare moments when it is deserved.

What my students, indeed all BEd. primary students, need is a range of experience which promotes a different sense of 'standards' from those they encounter in the narrow practicism of so many of their courses and which encourages a broader conception of roles than the mother-figure, cosy but firm, with the strangely emphatic voice, or the uncle-figure, track-suited and jocular. Personally, I prefer teachers like Olga. I take comfort from my music colleagues who took a party of students to India last year to study Indian musical techniques. I share the outrage of my art colleagues at the visual illiteracy promoted by so much 'display' in colleges and schools – the notion of 'Art' characterized by Maurice Rubens as 'out of trash can into the trash can' and which plasters corridors with inept concoctions of cotton wool, paper doilies and pasta.

I believe we underestimate these 'infantilist' pressures and their disastrous long term consequences for the personality of the teacher. But I do believe it is possible to avoid the divided personality of Mrs Perfect which, taught to mistrust its own powers as a learner, denies those for whom it is responsible. I think we can detect a more 'integrated' personality in these reflections by one of my fourth year students writing about the responses of some of the second year junior pupils she worked with last year. Their inner-city classroom became Prospero's island for six weeks as they developed a version of *The Tempest*. In this extract she is writing about the curses they wrote and the effect of Shakespeare's language on them:

> The fact that they identified, perhaps, with Caliban or his situation, motivated the children to devise some imaginative curses and insults. The extent of their knowledge of language and its uses was quite remarkable .... The power of Shakespeare's themes does get to the heart of our humanness and demonstrates the reality of our own experiences. The curses indicated the intensely personal input in their creation, for example, 'Thy body will be filled with an emptiness that nobody will be able to fill', is a realistic 'horrific' curse thought of with care and deliberation, as is ... 'May you be taunted by flickering flames around thee. Then the water that puts out these flames will be filled with tarantulas and black widow spiders. Not to kill thee, but to kill thy daughter, so thou shalt live in horror for the rest of thy life'. Here the child has captured the punishment that will hurt Prospero the most ....

Here, for all the imperfections, is a student who can reflect in the way I mentioned earlier and who will be an 'intellectual of a kind'.

9   How English teachers make themselves

Changing styles of English teaching

Initial training is only the first step in the making of English teachers. To a great extent they make and remake themselves throughout their professional careers. It is no longer possible - if it ever was – to go on teaching the same things in the same way, year after year, or to imagine that once trained a teacher can go on running smoothly for forty years with an occasional topping-up of oil and water. Even the youngest in our sample were aware that their perceptions of English and their classroom practices had already undergone changes, and for most of the teachers those changes had been profound. This chapter considers how, in an uncertain educational climate, English teachers are continually learning and remaking themselves. Particularly in the later sections, it also examines what they feel they need in order to develop fully as professionals.

When asked what changes they had observed in their own teaching only a very small minority reported that 'nothing has changed'; the more representative response was: 'My teaching has changed *radically*', 'enormously', or 'dramatically'. One said that after twenty-five years in school her teaching had altered 'so much and in so many ways' that it would need a book to outline what had taken place. Their views of these changes illustrate the implicit values that are acquired by belonging to one particular cultural group – English teachers – and by being involved in their work. Tony Becher has shown how 'differences in the basic values that different disciplines espouse' are revealed, particularly in 'their common terms of praise or blame'.[1] That is certainly true here. The responses show teachers making evaluative distinctions between what they perceive as 'good practice' in English and what is now thought to be outmoded or undesirable, and their choice of terminology is highly significant.

The changes they notice in themselves repeatedly contrast two groups of words or phrases. Former teaching styles that had been abandoned are described as 'authoritarian', 'autocratic', 'teacher-dominated' or 'teacher-orientated'; the rejected roles are those of the 'lecturer' or 'solo performer', the 'transmission model', or 'performer model'. Those terms can be set against such descriptions of present (and thus more favoured) practice as a 'group member', 'enabler', 'facilitator', 'partner' or 'agent of children's learning'; one who is 'child-centred', 'more engaged with pupils' or 'more accountable' to them. The teachers who employed these phrases span the whole age and experience range. This suggests that a radical change has been taking place in many English classrooms. In the former situation teachers were in control of all that went on during a lesson (the 'up-front model', as one expressed it), whereas they now see themselves as members of the learning group, rather than its director, sharing with pupils in giving direction to the lessons. One teacher in his 30s said:

> I no longer see myself as a missionary transmitting the light of my knowledge but as someone with respect for what children bring to lessons. My role is, to use the clichés, more one of facilitator, guide, confidant, audience, *et al.* I still see English as liberating, but in terms of developing autonomy and critical awareness – skills and attitudes rather than bodies of knowledge, human beings in complex social interactions rather than spirits to be nurtured.

Such changes have not taken place overnight, but as the result of a series of related shifts in curriculum, organization, methodology and principle. One head of English who has taught for twenty-seven years sums up the change:

> I began teaching as the 'creative writing' movement was affecting the grammar/comprehension/essay/classic literature model. This gave way to mixed ability and group talk with first moves towards 'negotiating' individual learning. I welcomed the 'thematic' mode which affected my lesson-planning for a long time and – eventually – beginning to understand children's development as readers affected my work with books. I think my teaching now shows the marks of all these 'movements'.

In the past, the preferred way of retaining pupils' interest and of arousing enjoyment and commitment was to be what people called the 'star turn', the 'solo performer', 'a Miss Jean Brodie charismatic'. One said: 'I think I viewed English as an "inspirational affair" – the teacher would communicate her love of literature to an appreciative student audience'. A more 'child-centred' approach, working through dialogue or 'interchange', draws out and then builds on the pupils' own interests and enjoyment.

> I used to think of it as an opportunity of conveying my enthusiasms to the pupils. Now I see the priority as using the pupils' own enthusiasms as the basis for work. I let them follow their own interests within a clear framework which I have set.

It is clear from the tone of the majority of these responses that successful teachers welcome and enjoy their present style ('now more child-centred, less performance, more relaxed, less frenetic') and that some of them distance themselves from the people they used to be. At the same time, however, a few experienced teachers suggest a measure of regret that the model of the great classroom performer is seen as less appropriate in present circumstances, and others feel that they have not radically adapted the principles and methods with which they began. One head of English in his 40s, for example, says:

As a product (I don't like this expression, but let it pass) of O'Malley – Thompson – *Use of English* teachers and taught by Leavis sympathizers at university, I went into teaching with those assumptions. They have become modified, but on the whole I am still, roughly speaking, a *Use of English* man.

Experienced teachers who made a conscious change seem to have found the new style 'more challenging and stimulating'; their practice has become 'less rigid' and 'more adventurous'. They say, for example, that 'now I will experiment with new ideas/books', 'I take risks', 'I am much more adventurous with material'. With experience, adaptability leads to increased confidence. Typical responses from teachers in mid-career attested 'I am so much more confident and therefore relaxed', 'my teaching is now more spontaneous, flexible and successful', 'I am much more relaxed [and] can enjoy it', 'more relaxed, more conversational … more flexible, more fun'.

An inevitable component of such change is a different kind of relationship with classes. One says, 'because I am more relaxed the children relax too and begin to assume that work is a natural part of lessons and not something that is done grudgingly'. Several teachers relatively new to the profession describe their surprise and relief in being able to establish a working atmosphere of this kind in which discipline no longer seems a problem.

Changing the organization of children's learning

The shift in focus described above means that teachers are thinking less of classes as units: 'English teaching, I now see, is to do with individual children'. One teacher of twenty-five years' experience described this change of emphasis in terms of a familiar dichotomy: 'My teaching is now pupil-oriented, not subject-oriented'. Understanding of real needs comes not from impersonal diagnosis but from a developing relationship through which the teacher is 'nurturing individual development appropriate to particular needs as they are revealed by the child'. Classroom approaches will often have to be 'individualized, experiential', and 'draw on pupils' *own* knowledge and understanding'. Of course, attempting to meet the needs of a roomful of individuals can also mean that 'more pressure is placed on staff'.

Such reactions are in part an embodiment of the influential 'growth' paradigm of English teaching: 'I am now more caring towards individuals', 'I give pupils their "own" space', 'pupils have greater personal freedom than the ones I taught ten or more years ago'. More frequently in these responses, though, teachers see their relationships changing because they are concerned to train pupils to make informed choices and to take on responsibilities. They comment, for instance, that 'there is now more emphasis on individual student responsibility for choice, negotiation and personal learning management' or 'the focus is far more on self-directed learning'.

How do these teachers see children as learning in their classrooms? The emphasis is on active engagement: 'Before the pupils were passive, now they are informed and actively involved with their learning'. A number felt that children were working harder than previously, because they were being challenged to think rather than carrying out activities unquestioningly. 'There is a much greater understanding of, and emphasis on, process'. Whereas teachers might once have assumed that pupils would recognize what and how they were learning, a 'major breakthrough' is discovering 'how to make explicit that which is sometimes assumed always to be gained implicitly'. Consequently, as one writes, 'I attempt to get levels of understanding more explicit. I talk explicitly, for example, about cooperative learning strategies'.

Teachers were well aware of the ways in which these wider educational changes had demanded corresponding changes in their planning. For example, 'the need for differentiation in mixed ability English means that I spend far more time thinking about my lessons before and after I've taught them'. The introduction of GCSE coursework, which gave teachers the freedom to choose texts, activities and written outcomes also required from them a more considered planning in which the different English activities were integrated. Teachers commented that 'work is more organized with GCSE than with O level'; 'I now plan lessons over a much longer period of time and deliver the work in "modules" lasting about five weeks each'; 'I think the changes in GCSE mean it is more difficult to switch to automatic pilot'.

The terminology chosen by our group of teachers is again significant here. On the one hand they praise the 'freedom', 'variety', 'range' and 'diversity' available to English teachers. Simultaneously, though, they see the need for English programmes to have 'structure', 'coherence', 'organization' and 'sequence'. What seems to matter is the source of that structure. Many of the teachers saw government pressures as one of the chief obstacles to effective teaching, feeling that their autonomy was under threat from the National Curriculum: 'there is more emphasis now on structured plans to fit *imposed* models'. Many of them record their resentment at the way that power over the curriculum has passed from teachers to bodies perceived as having little knowledge or experience of children or schools. 'I resent uninformed interference', says one, and others complain about 'the superstructure of largely ineffectual (but consistent) attempts at DES control' or 'the demands of ... new initiatives which leave us *exhausted*'. Alongside a general picture of English teachers approaching lesson planning thoughtfully and enthusiastically, then, we have to record this accompanying sense of idealism frustrated by lack of time for planning and evaluating lessons (just one of numerous constraints discussed in a later section of this chapter).

Changing curriculum practice

Teachers' perceptions of how the nature of English teaching had changed inevitably related pedagogical changes to shifts in the curriculum. When asked what were the most urgent problems facing English teachers at this time, nearly six out of ten mentioned the National Curriculum (considerably more references than for any other topic). Asked what changes they expected to see in the 1990s, more of our group (seven out of ten) referred to curricular developments than to anything else. One detailed reply from a head of English in a comprehensive school described how he had 'sought quite consciously to renew' his views of the nature of English teaching and his practice throughout his career, which had ranged 'from residual Denys Thompson and Raymond O'Malley in the mid-1960s to adventures in structuralism, semiotics and feminism in the 1980s'. We briefly illustrate here some of the most frequently mentioned changes, remaking ideas of what is appropriate in English lessons. In considering their own evolving practice, one recurrent theme is the new centrality of talk in the English curriculum; the fact that work in English must be 'led by talk'; the need to 'raise the status of talk in the classroom'. A third of our respondents chose to record as significant the fact that pupils now spend a greater proportion of their time in class involved in talk, mainly with their partners or in groups, and 'language between pupil and teacher is freer than before', according to one teacher of thirty years' experience. One result is that the activities of writing and reading have taken on a different character:

- I make different demands on pupils – less written work, more assessed 'activities'.

- I am demanding less written work – more involved with the oral process than just written product.

- We do less writing, far more talking and thinking.

It is notable that the most experienced teachers in our sample were very clear about this shift in emphasis. After thirty years in the profession, one records 'I spend more time doing oral English than ever before'. After twenty-seven years another says that 'the advent of group talk changed my practice and my classrooms' and after twenty years a third says 'I do a little more oral work now – not much more, as we have always talked a lot in my classes'.

There is also a different view of the role of talk in the classroom. In the early days of CSE the assumption seemed to be made that children would use spoken language for some kind of performance: to give a prepared talk, to undertake a prepared interview or to participate in an improvisation. The performance element is still present in contemporary classrooms, but the very act of talking and listening is now seen as important in itself and 'as a tool of learning'. 'Discussion, groupwork and oracy are now integral parts of the lesson', and where children are learning to become better talkers 'there is greater emphasis on talking and listening *skills*'.

Some respondents were not unaware that a classroom full of busily talking children is not necessarily one where the intended learning is taking place. An advisory teacher able to observe classrooms in a more detached way than the teachers busily involved there comments on

... the widespread belief that because language (particularly speaking and listening) is taking place throughout the curriculum then progression must be assured. This is simply not true. Although children are talking in pairs and small groups all over the place (one trips over them in cloakrooms) very few teachers are paying enough attention to *how* they should be developing and progressing through talk.

The chief change teachers record in their approaches to children's writing is an increased emphasis on drafting and revision. One young teacher describes enthusiastically the effect that this has had on her pupils:

> I expect pupils to rough draft without having to be told every time. I see it as the obvious way to work now, whereas when I started I felt that I was being expected to train 4th and 5th years to pass exams. Now I feel that I am helping to produce WRITERS (brilliant ones too!) rather than successful exam candidates.

Although teachers have been encouraged to develop drafting for some years, those who comment on its importance for them seem to have been influenced less by books for teachers (Donald Graves and others), classroom materials (like *From Rough to Best*, 1982) or even the National Writing Project, than by the coming of GCSE. Responses 'welcome' this emphasis as integral to coursework, and praise 'the value of drafting and all coursework approaches to enable pupils to demonstrate in the best possible conditions just what they can do'. As a result of discovering its value at this level, many teachers have found that 'Drafting at GCSE has "filtered down" to affect lower school work'.

It may be significant that comparatively few record any similar significant changes in the organization of reading activities, except to suggest increased emphasis on independent reading in and out of classrooms. Some teachers suggest that it is now more difficult to turn children into 'real readers', and assume that 'literature is a struggle with some because ... of the decline in reading generally'. Many say that the root of the problem is inadequate funds ('few books, capitation slashed 50 per cent for the past two years'). A third of the respondents who were asked what prevented them from teaching as they wished mentioned lack of resources, and a number specifically referred to difficulties in providing class libraries and in permitting children to take books home.

For one or two, however, the most profound changes in practice had come about as a result of questioning the term *literature* itself, and moving towards a wider interpretation of 'texts'. One said:

> The major change for me between 1966, when I started teaching, and today is an extension from an exclusive concentration on printed texts and the encouragement of written response in the form of essays and context/comprehension questions to an engagement with a wide variety of texts from the Nescafé jar to *King Lear*, from *Robin of Sherwood* to *Full Metal Jacket*, and an encouragement of pupil responses in a wide variety of modes.

Changing styles of assessment

The changing position of English as a subject and the changing situation of English teachers have always been intimately related to systems of assessment.

Seventy years ago it was the weight attached to English in the School Certificate that 'favourably affected its position in many schools', by making it one of five or six subjects taken by boys and girls up to age 16. The recognition by the Board of Education of English as one of the main subjects that could be taken for advanced courses in modern studies was described as 'another forward step of first-rate importance'.[2] The Newbolt Report explained later:

> We are anxious to encourage in every way the institution in schools of Advanced Courses with English as a main subject, because we believe that the inclusion of English as a subject in which specialisation is possible reacts favourably on the teaching of English throughout the school and will make it easier to secure well-qualified teachers to undertake it. (Para. 125)

The irony is that of all subject teachers, those concerned with English have expressed the strongest opposition to examinations, and yet the present importance of the subject is largely due to examination demands: the fact that more students pass GCSE English than any other subject, the astonishing rise in popularity of English Literature over a thirty year period, and the A-level situation in which English (alongside mathematics) dominates the curriculum.[3]

It has to be said that the modes of assessment in English – as in other subjects – have frequently had a harmful effect on teaching and curriculum because what has been tested has had little to do with the real nature of the subject.[4] However, it could reasonably be suggested that genuinely new approaches to English for all pupils have gone hand-in-hand with changes in the examination system. The successive movements from O-level to GCSE have organizationally broken down the divisions between groups of pupils in different kinds of school, or in the same school. A new unity of English teachers and new approaches to English teaching became inevitable as soon as all children from an area were in one school and the responsibility of one English department. As classroom methods have developed to focus attention on pupils learning rather than on teachers teaching, so the function and methods of assessment have changed. From the evidence of our sample, the current emphasis on assessment as an integral part of the teaching and learning process has been hastened in particular by the introduction of coursework assessment in GCSE (and for some at A-level) and of records of achievement.

The emphasis on positive evaluation in both of these has clearly pervaded assessment at all levels. Three teachers, each with fifteen years' experience, pick this out as the major change in their practice: 'I try to be positive ("can do" model)'; 'I tend to approach their work from a positive point of view rather than see it as work which has *not* reached a particular level'; assessment is totally different 'from grades/marks to positive comments as a reader of children's work'. The last of these sees a shift in role, from being assessor and examiner to being a 'reader', adviser and co-worker. Assessment as part of a two-way process between teacher and pupil is one of the key elements in the recording of achievements. In order to help children to become aware of their own progress, teachers have to help them realize what they are aiming for in any given assignment and also to increase their understanding of how far those aims have been attained. There is no point in a marking code which is meaningful for teachers but obscure for pupils. The references are to a shared diagnostic and 'negotiated' process: 'I now talk about marking strategies with students'.

Although respondents generally expressed enthusiasm for changes like these, there was also considerable concern about what might follow. Looking into the future from 1990, nearly half of them referred to assessment as one of those areas where they anticipated further major change, and in some cases their references were in terms of 'fear'. Over a third of the teachers named the pressures of assessment as one of the 'most urgent problems' now facing them. For example, the successful implementation of records of achievement requires (but is not allocated) time for negotiation with pupils, and makes heavy administrative and class-management demands on the teacher. As one said, 'There is an increased need for sophisticated management/admin. strategies to deal with current demands, especially profiles/self-assessment'. Supporters of positive self-assessment are concerned that these principles may be put at risk by the demands of National Curriculum testing. Although the declared function of such testing is diagnostic, many felt that the bald assignment to ten levels was at odds with negotiated self-assessment.

Although continuous assessment at GCSE level is virtually universally welcomed, some teachers are acutely aware of the dangers and difficulties involved. As the grading of oral and written work is a necessary process in an externally examined course, the formative role can too easily be left aside. Teachers can be pushed back into being 'examiners' rather than 'readers'. In addition, perhaps as a by-product of teachers' conscientiousness, there is a temptation to assess everything that pupils write. As one young teacher suggests: 'the treadmill of GCSE coursework leaves very little time for experimental teaching. Texts and assignments are constantly being rushed through and the completed folder has become a fetish'. Another similarly commented on the pressure towards 'formula teaching', saying, 'I underestimated the systematic (almost!) assembly-line potential of GCSE in particular, e.g. textual stimulus – oral response – written assignment'.

Constraints on effective professional development

A recurrent theme in the responses to our enquiry is the sense of frustration from teachers who are anxious to improve their practice but who feel that they are being hampered by pressures from outside and from within the school. As will be suggested by the comments quoted in this section, they feel overstretched by a series of new 'initiatives' (especially the National Curriculum and its assessment), by the variety of roles they are called on to fulfil and by their marking and record-keeping load. The problem is exacerbated by failings in school organization, in staffing and in accommodation and resources. In such a situation, their own professional development seems to be pushed on one side.

When asked what they saw as 'the most urgent problems facing English teachers', their overwhelming response was to name either the National Curriculum or, in one form or another, pressure, stress and lack of time. Women were proportionately more likely to mention the latter than men, and the under-40s more than the over-40s. The simple phrase 'lack of time' is repeated over and over again as the chief obstacle to teaching as one would wish, alongside 'overload', 'pressure of work', 'overwork', 'workload' and 'stress'.

Teachers lament 'the lack of time to do *anything* properly', 'the lack of opportunity to think about *how* to teach and lack of time to spend with children', 'not enough time to prepare lessons as well as I'd like', 'limited opportunities for reflection, evaluation', lack of time 'to do all that is required'. One said simply that 'time is the chief problem – there is often so much paperwork that inspiration has to take a back seat, as does the preparation of resources'. What they most need is 'time to prepare, assimilate, think', 'the time to develop initiatives', 'the motivation to work as effectively as the job requires', 'the provision of time and space to put current ideas into practice in the classroom', 'space to think about ends rather than means'. In what different ways do these pressures manifest themselves?

English teachers today have to fulfil several different roles, and many saw these as taking time and energy away from the main business of subject teaching, especially for those in positions as head of department or deputy head. When asked if their expertise as English teachers had been used in school outside the classroom, the responses indicate that in addition to traditional out-of-school English activities (28 per cent involved with drama and productions; 14 per cent with school magazines), many were serving in other ways: chairing or taking minutes at meetings, writing or proof-reading whole-school documents, promoting cross-curricular activities or leading activities in school in-service programmes.

Internal demands of this kind are increasing alongside external initiatives that generate more work for individual teachers as well as for their departments. The introduction of GCSE, Key Stage three of the National Curriculum and records of achievement have all required an increase in record-keeping, most of which must be completed outside the classroom. The notorious preparation and marking load in English is still rarely acknowledged. One teacher demanded, 'Has anyone ever compared how much we have to read with other subjects?' When asked what they thought differentiated English teachers from their colleagues in other subjects, one in five cited the difference in marking load. There is confirmatory evidence in the survey that these demands have increased as a result of coursework assessment for GCSE and (in some cases) for A-level. Despite enthusiasm for the principle, three respondents use the term 'treadmill' to describe the unending flow of GCSE marking. Allocated 'non-contact' time is rarely free for marking: 'often during school time the free lessons are lost on cover or sorting out a problem which has arisen during the day'.

Many respondents comment on the consequent pressure on 'non-directed' time: 'Five nights a week I spend six p.m. to twelve p.m. on marking and preparation'. References to this pressure recur in the advice they offer to prospective English teachers: 'be prepared to put some limits on your time'; 'find out *exactly* what it entails in terms of marking, work to be done in evenings and own time'; 'be prepared to have to work very hard, but make sure you make time for yourself or you'll have nothing to give'; 'don't expect to have a social life outside school and get a sympathetic partner'. Asked what alternative career respondents would choose, one replied '*anything* with less marking'. An English adviser writes that what she has gained from her new post is 'no more acres of marking, with no respite'. Under such pressure, English teachers are forced into having to make invidious distinctions about their priorities. 'The demands of coursework for GCSE and A-level are enormous and I constantly feel under pressure at having to choose where my priorities lie between different classes, preparation or materials and marking etc.'.

The pressure on time is intensified by what many see as poor school organization. 'The main obstacle is everything on the periphery, e.g. admin., form tutor things, endless meetings'. 'Management' in school is often thought unhelpful because of 'head teachers who do not understand the nature of English teaching', who put 'administrative convenience' before effective teaching, or impose rigid systems into which teachers have to fit. Comments are made on the way that 'we experience restriction from "management"', on the head's 'attempts to straitjacket the curriculum', and on 'poor' management that makes English teachers the victims of 'admin. hiccups'. A number of teachers referred to the way in which administrative duties and assessment tasks during lessons diminish the time 'to talk to individuals'. Necessary in-service preparation for the steady stream of 'initiatives' during the 1980s and 1990s 'takes time away from the classroom'. The introduction of 'directed time' as part of teachers' contracts seems to have encouraged some head teachers and their teams to increase the number of meetings rather than directing the time more productively. Several respondents predicted that the requirement to explore cross-curricular themes within the National Curriculum would add further demands.

The organization of lesson time within school timetables has always been a source of tension (and sometimes of dissent) between English departments and administrators. This survey suggests that there is still widespread dissatisfaction with the length and frequency of periods and with failures to 'block' English teachers together. Some are more profoundly dissatisfied with the rigid structures of secondary school timetabling – 'hour periods and bells' – and the effects of this on any attempts to cross curriculum boundaries. 'There is too much compartmentalization and an inability therefore to develop thematic project work that needs larger blocks of time'. Moreover, there is a constantly repeated fear that the actual curriculum time devoted to English will be reduced under pressure from competing subject areas under the National Curriculum. The most urgent problems for several teachers were 'holding on .to adequate classroom time for English' or 'fighting for time for English in the curriculum'.

For years English has occupied, on average, 12.5 per cent of the secondary week, but models advanced by the National Curriculum Council and by some local authorities have assumed only 10 per cent. Several respondents complained of cuts that had already been made on this assumption: 'Number of lessons for English slashed by a fifth'.

'Radical' changes in classroom practice have not been accompanied by changes in the buildings where the work goes on, and frustration with the limitations of the environment is frequently expressed. Small, bare rooms filled with desks facing the blackboard may have been acceptable for an earlier generation, but they are inadequate for the current emphasis on group and individual learning with varied activities and teaching styles deploying a range of materials and media. There are too many 'inflexible teaching areas'; 'poor, cramped, echoing rooms which hamper group work'; 'nowhere to send small groups for recording, etc.'; 'nowhere for drama'. Respondents comment on the poor and inappropriate furniture and on the lack of resources that National Curriculum orders seem to assume are freely available in all schools. 'There is no money for computers'; 'no money for word-processors in our rooms and the wrong lay-out if we did have them'.

Such strong dissatisfaction with aspects of their working lives reveals teachers conscious of struggling against forces that hinder them from achieving the best for their pupils. (It is notable that their own pay is not advanced as a constraint.)

In-service provision for English

It is a commonplace that good English teachers are also good learners. In precisely the same way that teaching and research are seen to go hand in hand for academics, so do they in teaching. The difference is simply in the kind of continuous learning that goes on in the classroom, which teachers are often reluctant to dignify with the name of 'research', because it may not result in a formal qualification or in publication. However, nobody who has seen as many small-scale studies and papers emerging from English teaching as we have can doubt their significance as an extension of teachers' understanding and expertise. At the level of more formal qualifications, it is striking that over half of our group had gained additional degrees and diplomas, and that they rated further academic study very highly as a factor in their development.

It is very worrying, then, to consider what little inducement in terms of released time, or financial reward, or even simple encouragement is currently offered to those who wish to equip themselves better for their work. The general lack of concern for an adequately qualified teaching force, accompanied by a particular view that qualifications in English are somehow less significant than in other curricular subjects, is mirrored in the patterns of in-service provision. Achieving in this sense any improvement in teacher quality is a lengthy process.

It took thirty years after the last war to increase the proportion of graduates in the teaching force from 16 per cent to 28.3 per cent.[5] The James Committee (1972) recognized the vital importance of providing continuing education and training throughout a professional career, and recommended that at any time 3 per cent of all teachers should be released for further study, rising as soon as possible to 5 per cent.[6] In fact, full-time release never rose above 1 per cent., and even that seems utopian in the present climate.

General restrictions on finance, the cancelling of the 'pool' system after 1986, and a policy of putting funds first into the hands of local authorities as 'employers' and then into the schools have virtually killed off full-time advanced study extending for a year. Greeting these new arrangements with pleasure, one LEA adviser for in-service education remarked that such courses had always been a waste of money, because as soon as teachers got their advanced degrees they gained promotion in other authorities. Such narrow-minded and short-sighted views have contributed to a situation in which full-time secondments have dropped to a seventh of what they were two years earlier, and recruits for research degrees in education dropped almost to zero.[7] Individual teachers no longer have access to financial support for courses leading to higher qualifications. Many heads are seriously underspending their delegated training budgets and failing to release staff from school to attend courses.[8] At present there is a clear mis-match between teachers' perceptions of essential in-service provision and the views of the 'providers' (the DES, local authorities and – in some cases – school management). Respondents had little or nothing good to say about the short 'priority area' courses that have replaced extended study, the quick fixes to meet new policies. 'From my experience of INSET', said one, 'I would much rather the money had been spent on books and materials for my students'. 'I would very much like to have a year with NO INSET', said another. They did *not* want 'heaps of role play', or 'one-off lectures', or people who 'apologize saying they know very little about the course subject and what do *you* want to do over the next six meetings'. Too few felt that teachers' own assessments of their professional needs were being taken into account. Genuine professional development only comes about when it is grounded in a particular teacher's awareness of a need and a desire to meet it.

What they most wanted can be quickly summed up. First they wanted time free from regular demands; what one called 'sabbatical time'. Within the school they wished for 'time to work with colleagues on specific schemes/areas of work, and to read'; 'time to sit down with colleagues and produce realistic and coherent programmes of study'; 'opportunity to work with other teachers, to share their experiences'; 'supply cover so that I could team teach with those I would like to influence'. More widely, they would welcome 'more time to meet departments from other schools – sharing, collaborating'; 'experience of other schools'; 'meetings with other heads of department'; courses 'made up of teachers from other schools, where the agenda is set by teachers'.

Second, many would like such time to be spent specifically in developing resources and schemes of work. They mention favourably 'courses which provide resources for the classroom', 'groups of teachers across schools (and phases) planning and developing resources'; courses 'that deal with the preparation of realistic materials … ideas and approaches that have been found to be successful are always useful'; 'school-focused, school-based development of materials, supported by LEA advisers offering time and support'.

Third, many still hope for courses that will provide an 'external stimulus' for their English teaching. They say, for example, 'I need regular recharging', 'new ideas to stimulate fresh approaches', 'refresher courses about the subject and the teaching of it, to revitalize one', 'demonstrations/involvement in "good practice" to widen my horizons'. One suggested that 'any courses are useful as long as they are active rather than just lectures'. Although some emphasize 'specific lessons, not theory', 'practices which you can take back to the classroom', others perceive their needs in terms of 'being kept up with recent research', 'a chance to do research and develop my own ideas', 'in-school research and feedback'. There is a wistful note in some responses, yearning for 'secondment for an MA course', more HMI courses ('a week like that every year would be wonderful'), or 'high powered conferences'. One teacher in his 40s envisaged a policy suggested in the James Report, 'an entitlement to a long-term period of study, say a term or more away from the classroom, every five years, so that you know that it's coming and can plan it as part of your career development'.

In recent years, in-service provision for English teachers has been particularly unfavourable. Funds earmarked by the government have been allocated for fashionable concerns like information technology, science teaching, economic awareness and special needs. Local authorities have tended to concentrate on authority-wide topics like organization and management or personal and social development. Despite its key role in the National Curriculum, English has been substantially ignored. When the teachers in the survey were asked an open question about the kinds of course they would personally welcome, their overwhelming response was to name particular aspects of the English curriculum. Indeed, the only other topic seriously mentioned was management of one kind or another ('the more functional "business" side of teaching is becoming increasingly important' asserted a young teacher). Courses on English in the National Curriculum, on reading, knowledge about language, media studies, information technology in English, literature teaching at A-level and mixed-ability English teaching were most mentioned, but every area of the English curriculum was proposed by some teachers. It is clear that these needs have been outrageously ignored in many parts of the country.

All this has laid an even heavier responsibility on the English department itself as a training agency, establishing its own links with other schools, with universities and colleges and with advisory teams. Significantly, heads of English in many areas are now coming together to formulate their in-service needs and to explore ways of meeting them. In the next section, we briefly consider the role of the department itself as a training agency.

The department as training agency

English teachers see other English teachers as a major influence on their own development. After initial preparation, with its concentration on developing an individual teaching personality and becoming an independent practitioner, the department becomes the next training institution, with the head of department taking on some of the functions of a tutor (and being seen as a particularly important influence by the younger teachers in our sample). Probationers rapidly realize that their colleagues, far from threatening their autonomy, have ideas and expertise which can support them. As one puts it: 'Without a collaborative department my work would be impossible, so I am now conscious of the need to function as a department member and not as an isolated individual'.

For a more experienced and confident teacher the head of department is seen as one of a team of colleagues and not a solo replacement trainer. 'I'm now a better teacher because I've investigated good practice among colleagues', says one. Good practice is shared through example, discussion, working together and the sharing of resources, and at its best the department can be its own in-service team. This point is made by several department heads. Asked about their in-service needs they list as a priority for training days that the English department should work together, rather than being involved in 'spurious' whole-school INSET events.

A recent research study suggests that the relative success of schools is largely determined by the quality of management at this departmental level. The effective department head is one who regards in-service training as central, who can create 'the sort of climate or ethos in which people – and the curriculum – could develop'. The ability to create a team was found to be the dominant characteristic. 'Teachers within effective departments felt secure, freely expressed opinions, constructively criticized each other's practices and were not reluctant to admit possible weaknesses'.[9] Those in our sample who are no longer teaching in schools look back to this aspect of departmental life with regret. The relative isolation they feel as lecturers or advisers leads them to value the 'sense of working with others', the 'team work' and 'the support of a good English department'. One advisory teacher remembers the way in which working together develops friendship: 'I miss the daily companionship of a close-knit group of English teachers, "Hey, have you read this?", "Look at Gary's poem", etc.'. The nostalgia is balanced by the realism of another advisory teacher's final comment: 'I miss working with a "team" that had common aims and was developing practice together (not very common!)'.

The evidence from within schools that this experience is 'not very common' is revealed in the comments of some heads of English who are struggling to create the 'close-knit group' or 'team' so fondly remembered by others. A number of effective teachers responding to the questionnaire find themselves having to work with colleagues whose expertise they feel is inadequate or whose morale is low. One respondent complained that 'as head of department too much energy is going into supporting weak colleagues', largely because 'there are too many non-specialists (fourteen of us doing the job nine full time English teachers could do)'. The same person also comments on the frustration caused by teachers jockeying for too few incentive allowances. To lead a department in such circumstances ('the greatest obstacle is lack of sympathetic commitment in the department') can give rise to feelings of isolation and frustration. The ideal may be of a departmental team sharing on an equal basis, but the reality is frequently a hierarchical one, with the majority stuck on the main professional grade. 'Excellent MPG teachers with experience have no chance of career advancement'. For present heads of English the task of creating departmental teams seems complex and fraught at a time when cooperation and the sharing of responsibilities seems more important than it has ever been. We still lack a structure that really rewards those who genuinely seek opportunities for self-development and who make themselves – and others – into effective English teachers.

10 Conclusion: making it better

It is clear that we need to be better, not only in Britain, at recruiting good English teachers, at equipping and renewing them for their work, and at retaining them in the classroom. There seems little doubt that this task has been made harder by the continual attacks on teachers, schools and teacher education, which have devalued the profession and lowered the status of those who teach. What sort of measures might make English teaching more attractive as a career-long profession? Money is part of the answer, certainly. Higher salaries and longer and better-funded professional preparation might enable us to attract more applicants, to be more selective in choosing future teachers and to equip them better for their work. It was striking, however, that our respondents were not obsessed (as they might well have been) with the inadequate rewards offered to them. They were more concerned with those other forces that prevented them from becoming fully professional, and it is with these that we will be chiefly concerned here.

This book has given reasons for believing that effective English teachers are highly committed to equipping themselves for their vocation. In brief, they wish for greater professional autonomy and for better opportunities for professional development. Their perception is that programmes of teacher education are more effective now than they were in the past. They hope for further improvements, but wholly reject any ideas of major structural change. The belief that we share with these teachers is that the brake on further progress has been applied by the so-called 'reforms' introduced from outside during the doctrinaire decade of the 1980s, with its paranoid mistrust of professional opinion and of the 'education establishment'. It also has to be admitted that the beliefs held by our sample are not universal; that forces within the profession as well as outside it have too often been resistant to change.

We have seen that the inherent conservatism of the educational system made the establishment of English as a subject slow and difficult and also ensured that changes in curriculum, assessment and methodology came slowly. Looking back forty years to his first book, Sir Philip Hartog reflected gloomily in 1947 that there had been little change in general classroom practice in English teaching, that the ideas he had advanced seemed no more established, that the same weaknesses in teaching methods remained.[1] The phrases in the Newbolt Report about teachers being 'unaware of or afraid of their liberty', welcoming 'the restrictions that no longer bind them' (para. 58) are echoed sixty years later in comments that 'teachers seem to have forged their own manacles'.[2]

Such insecure fear of the new has been fostered by ill-informed public opinion and by pressure from the media, opposing even modest proposals for change and making shock-horror allegations about falling standards. 'It is notorious that educational standards, and particularly literacy, seem to fall with such monotonous regularity from generation to generation that it is a wonder that anybody reads at all'.[3] At intervals throughout this century the voices raised against any change in approaches to English teaching have always sung the same tunes. Standards are falling, we are told, because rigour and accuracy are being abandoned in favour of self-expression and imagination; formal linguistic study and great literature are being driven out in the quest for easy, enjoyable activities. The laments over 'a general absence of the mental discipline formerly provided by a grounding in the essentials of Latin Grammar' (1926), the assertions that because of methods that 'foster emotionalism, introspection and self-thinking' (1929) writing is increasingly marked by 'muddled and slipshod expression, lack of punctuation and faults of grammar' (1930) were strident in the years following the Newbolt Report.[4] The complaints and the language in which they are expressed are indistinguishable from those of the Black Papers at the end of the 1960s and of the more recent Right-wing papers in the 1980s.

The similar pressures on teacher education have also resulted in an overemphasis on the status quo. Experimental courses do not fit neatly within the HMI/CATE check-list. In the past, studies of departments and faculties of education found them essentially traditional and reluctant to innovate. The conclusions a few years ago were almost despairing: 'The goals of faculties of education ... do not well equip them for change .... Such a climate is unlikely to produce the type of collaborative efforts required to initiate and sustain the change that is required for major reform .... Faculties are completely incapable of dealing with the changes which must come'.[5] Although, as we have seen in Chapters 5 to 8, change has been taking place, the formal system which now regulates the process and imposes one particular pattern on all institutions ensures that innovation will be limited.

What needs to be done?

We offer here some twenty proposals for improving the situation, arranged not in order of importance but in a rough sequence following the preceding chapters of this book.

- We need to increase professional awareness of the brief history of English studies. It is tempting for students to accept current views as somehow 'given', to concentrate on finding answers to the immediate problem. However, such answers only make sense within a historical and cultural context. Understanding depends on awareness of how ideas have developed, and particularly (as suggested above) of the way in which so many present arguments are simply re-running previous ones. Examining late nine-teenth-century hysteria about low standards of writing in the public schools gives a new perspective on John Marenbon. The furious debate over *English from 5 to 16* and the *Kingman Report* can be better understood in the light of reactions to the Newbolt Report: the obsession with 'discipline', with 'hard grind', with 'drill on fundamentals' including 'parsing and analysis'; the false antithesis between freedom and enjoyment, the expressive and imaginative on the one hand and 'disciplined language instruction', 'correctness' and 'standards' on the other.

- There is a corresponding need to raise awareness about the special difficulties that English teachers face in controlling the nature of their own subject. Beliefs about the nature of English, as Davies and Benton write in Chapter 6, have to be 'contested, explored and ultimately justified'. However, there are inevitable difficulties in preparing to teach a subject that contributes simultaneously to so many of the 'areas of experience' in the curriculum and that draws theoretical support from so many disciplines: the social sciences (particularly psychology and sociology), science (linguistics), the humanities (literature) and the arts (creativity and drama). Not only is there a continuing debate about what 'English' is (discussed in Chapters 1 and 9), professional opinion in English may conflict with assumptions that are widely touted in educational or governmental circles. The nature of English as a school subject is too easily made subsidiary to a generalized view of the curriculum or of organizational structures.[6] One example of this would be the attempt to super-impose managerial models and behavioural objectives on all subjects, even on those like English where they do not naturally fit.[7] Another would be the essentially conservative pressure to prepare students for the 'reality' of schools today, assuming that 'English' exists in roughly similar forms in different schools, and that the job of training is to help students to discover what is teachable in those places: the topics, activities and texts that will be appropri-ate there. Students are expected to endorse the principles and practices of the department they enter on teaching practice, or at least not to challenge them too openly.

- We need to explore ways of supporting English teachers against popular assumptions and prejudices. There are particular difficulties in our subject for maintaining professional knowledge and research evidence, because whereas few people feel competent to challenge expert opinion in physics or eco-nomics, say, the majority believe that they are qualified to pronounce about English and how it should be taught. Folk myths about language, writing and reading continue to influence classroom behaviour in the teeth of the evidence against them offered in training courses. Miles Olson has attempted to explain this in relation to other popular but irrational beliefs. He suggests that if society generally believes that it is necessary to know the parts of speech and to analyse sentences in order to write well, then 'it is a matter of *low* societal cost to practise what society believes and to perpetuate such practices'. Conversely, there is a '*high* cultural cost' in going against society's instinctive beliefs by implementing approaches that are based on research studies: 'because such research-based practices have the potential of eroding the popular wisdom, they are quickly rejected'.[8] Membership of local groups and of national organizations, as well as the support of a good department, may help to give young English teachers a sense of security.

- The supply of qualified English teachers must be improved. Not only should English be publicly acknowledged as the shortage subject that it is, but also the proportion of English taught by the non-qualified (which has hardly changed in recent decades) should be systematically reduced. There should be an immediate increase in the number of English graduates admitted to PGCE courses (where the academic standard of entrants is still reasonably high). Although we have doubts about the policy of offering bursaries to supplement inadequate grants in the hope of enticing graduates to enter teacher training, we certainly see no possible justification for offering these to chemists or modern linguists but not to students of English.

- We need to define more clearly just what is essential in the initial preparation of future English teachers. Our view is that English methodology should be the dominant element, and that the methods practised there should exemplify the kinds of teaching and learning we hope to see in secondary classrooms. One of the weaknesses of CATE's proposals is that they generalize across subjects, instead of admitting that different secondary specialists may require different treatment. (As one example, Colin Peacock shows in Chapter 7 how micro-teaching approaches favoured in some subjects are inappropriate for English; for another, the kinds of information technology most helpful for English are different from those most frequently offered in 'general' IT courses.) The result of this 'universalism' is an over-stuffed curriculum under continual pressure from interested groups claiming that *all* students should give more attention to 'their' topics. We offer token tastes of these to keep the critics quiet, but what increasingly gets squeezed out is perhaps the most important thing of all: time to reflect, evaluate and synthesize. Significantly, all who have written for this volume stress the importance of what Davies and Benton call, in Chapter 6, 'learning habits of reflectiveness that will survive the approaching pressures of full-time professionalism'. In addition, English students need the ability and the confidence, through experience, themselves to write poetry, to act, to improvise, to discuss emotive issues without embarrassment (and for some of them this will prove harder than any more academic demands) and these activities require time; confidence cannot be acquired overnight.

- The present impressionistic and anecdotal debates over teacher education demand to be stiffened with research evidence, especially as it is the government, not the profession, that now largely determines how new recruits will be inducted. It is quite extraordinary that the introduction of surveillance by bureaucratic bodies like CATE and its associated committees has been unaccompanied by any project to assess their influence. A small pilot study into the 'effectiveness' of teacher training courses, based on two institutions, is due to begin shortly, and we hope that that will swiftly be followed by much more sustained research, including some evaluation of licensed and articled teacher schemes.

- We believe that it is 'Time to stop hunting the teacher trainers', as *The Times Educational Supplement* editorial puts it, and to turn attention to the real problem: the failure to give new English teachers adequate support in their first posts.[9] HMI found that 'a substantial proportion of all schools were making no, or inadequate, provision for the needs of their new teachers', and pointed out that 'some aspects of training cannot be developed in depth until the probationer is in post'.[10] Although there are now national requirements for initial teacher education, no such requirements exist for induction, which has become a lottery. It would surely not be difficult to create an agreed framework for ways of building on what has been gained during the PGCE or BEd. course. At the least, new teachers should be assured of a reduced timetable that avoids notoriously difficult groups, a programme of release for meetings and training with other probationers within and outside the school, chances to observe as well as to be observed and to team-teach. We need to stress *entitlement* to support, to make the notion of induction a reality, and to stop imagining that any one-year professional course can be adequate preparation for full-time teaching. It is a shorter training period than for any other skilled profession. If the articled teacher scheme can take two years, there seems good reason to extend the principle further. A PGCE course based in a university or polytechnic, with extended periods in more than one school, followed by a year in school with periods of sharing, reflection and preparation back in the institution, might offer a better preparation for a career as an English teacher.

- We require much greater awareness (not only on the part of teachers) that professional competence depends on regular learning and up-dating. We have hardly begun to develop powerful incentives for English teachers to continue learning, to encourage them to meet in professional organizations, to continue reading periodicals and research reports, to experiment in their classrooms, rather than falling back on undemanding and outmoded methods and materials. How can they be helped to use (and, if necessary, to demand) opportunities for future growth? Knowledge about learning and about teaching increases all the time. One way of promoting development would be to make it financially advantageous. At present, the many teachers who give up time to gain additional qualifications are given no credit (let alone any increase in salary) for their efforts. We would do well to follow North American traditions here, and to expect that teachers will normally commit themselves to continuing study (accumulating 'credits' or completing successive 'modules') and to be rewarded for this. As we have pointed out that a high proportion of successful teachers had been members of the National Association for the Teaching of English, perhaps other authorities should follow the example of one which experimented with offering free membership of NATE to its English teachers.

- There is a need for research that poses questions about the serious under-representation of women in the advisory services and in teacher education, considering the high proportion of women in English teaching. We need a clearer understanding of the reasons why this should be so, and of the hidden messages that are transmitted to young women teachers. Is it possible that the situation becomes self-perpetuating because such women lack adequate role-models?

- We should strive to overcome the present discontinuity between many academic English courses in higher education and method work in the subject. Although the content of degree courses varies, the emphasis is generally strongly on works of English literature, which will occupy relatively little of a young teacher's time. The Kingman Committee pointed to the need for future teachers to experience courses in linguistics and the study of contemporary language, but many would also be helped by courses in children's literature, in speech and drama. The *nature* of the courses offered is much more important than the fact that an individual has completed two years of 'degree-level' study. We should be working for better liaison between English departments in schools and in universities and polytechnics. Such a need emerged clearly in the *Students of English* Research Project, where teachers and lecturers alike found such liaison desirable, but were less certain about what forms it should take.[11] One major step would be for more university English departments to offer options of particular help to those considering a career in teaching: children's literature, cultural studies, applied linguistics. Correspondingly, as at Stirling and at York, it would be helpful if some 'education' courses were available to students who were not intending to become teachers. Such steps have the additional benefit of breaking down artificial barriers between lecturers in English and in education (who should surely by now have established a joint organization).

- Lecturers in English in education should be better rewarded in terms of pay and promotion. At present it is absurd that successful school teachers cannot apply for posts in teacher education because the salary scales offered to new lecturers are frequently below those earned by a head of English in school. The old prejudices against education as a subject still live on. Years of effective work in school, an essential preparation for the post, are not seen as a significant qualification. Classroom based enquiries and curriculum development are not considered 'real' research. No allowance is made for the fact that education lecturers teach more weeks in the year and more hours in the week than most colleagues in other departments. There is increasing evidence that even when their research and publishing records are equal to those of people who have spent all their lives in higher education, education staff are discriminated against in promotion. If teacher education is to continue to improve, then the status of the subject and the working conditions it offers desperately need to be better.

- In schools, there is a manifest need for a different career structure, that does not drive talented English teachers away from the work they do so well in order to seek 'promotion'. As Marr and MacLure discovered in their ESRC project, it is not classroom work that gains an allowance for young teachers but extra responsibilities requiring time that might be given to English.[12] When heads of English take on school management posts, 'sadly, their English is seen as being of secondary importance'. 'There really should be incentive to stay in the classroom' (head of English); 'Classroom teachers need incentive to stay there' (advisory teacher of English). One possible structure would be to establish different professional grades (like American 'master' teachers) that are not dependent simply on accepting particular functions but also on a combination of length of experience and additional qualifications gained (either through responsibilities carried out, or through award-bearing courses, or through additional 'modular' short courses). We see no reason to assume that all three deputy heads in a comprehensive school should automatically receive a higher salary than the most experienced and best qualified heads of department. The present arrangement reinforces the damaging view that 'managing' in a school is somehow more important than teaching and training.
- If schools are to take a larger share in initial teacher preparation, then it is essential that the work of English students should be in the hands of teachers who are not simply good practitioners (important though that is), but who are also more widely informed about current research and developments in the English curriculum. Not all good classroom teachers are comfortable or competent in working with older students, and ideally specific training should be given to those who seem to be appropriate for this role. If the previous proposals were to be accepted, then it would be relatively simple to insist that a teacher-tutor should be qualified at a certain level as a 'senior' or 'master' teacher of English, and should be adequately rewarded for the work.
- Schools and training institutions should come to a clearer agreement about their collaborative responsibilities in preparing students for the classroom. Meetings of English teachers and lecturers at Hull have resulted in improved exchanges of information and in a precise statement about the complementary obligations of students, lecturers, teacher-tutors and professional tutors in school. An example of a more extensive, county-wide agreement is the document 'School experience and teaching practice in Nottinghamshire', which could well be adopted more widely.[13]
- If real 'partnership' between schools and training institutions is to become a reality, then there is a need for *consistent* contact between particular English tutors and schools: the 'mutually supportive relationships' described by

Anthony Adams in Chapter 5. It is surely unsatisfactory for students to be supervised on school experience by tutors who have not worked with them on subject methodology. It is also unsatisfactory for administrators to allocate English students in one year to different schools from those used in the previous year. Mutual trust and cooperative work can only come about when tutors are regularly in the same schools alongside the same teachers. From our experience, we believe that there are also great advantages when English students are placed in pairs in schools (as is also the practice at Oxford). Although this has been found to be successful by English teachers in schools and in the university, plans to extend this are regularly frustrated because they clash with the ideas of administrators within the institutions.

- The present fudging over the expenses of teacher involvement in training has to come to an end. At the moment, an indefensible system is being propped up through good will on both sides, but this will wear thin as Local Management of Schools becomes established. Teachers are sharing in interviews, joining in the teaching in universities and colleges and working with students in schools, frequently receiving no more than an occasional meal in return. Neither the schools nor departments of education can meet the real costs from their restricted budgets, and few authorities are as helpful as Oxfordshire have been (see Chapter 6). If thinking in the DES is that practising teachers should take a larger share in training, then the Department should fund this activity.

- In view of the insecurities expressed by advisory teachers of English, their role and their conditions of service should be regularized. At the moment there is no agreement about the length of secondment, the pay scales and conditions or the degree of autonomy offered by different authorities, and the situation is made worse because of the accompanying re-definition of existing advisory (or inspectorial) services. We see potential advantages for teams of advisory teachers, in providing 'credible' help for English staff, in offering a further career 'rung' for experienced practitioners, and in giving individuals a chance to widen their experience and their understanding. However, such advantages can only come about if there is more coherent national practice.

- In a climate where *entitlement* has become a favourite word, it is surely time to establish teachers' mandatory rights to periods of release for professional development. At present their contracts provide only for five non-contact days each year, and almost all respondents were highly critical of the use currently made of these. As a number of them suggested, the right to a period for study (a term every five or seven years, or the equivalent) is a very different matter from being dependent as at present on luck, favouritism or competition with others who are equally deserving. It was significant that those who had left the classroom for lecturing or advisory work almost all mentioned 'time to think' as one of the motives or benefits of making that move.

- The present haphazard system of INSET provision (called by one writer The Great In-service Training Robbery) needs to be replaced by a coordinated scheme in which due account is given to teachers' own formulation of their professional needs. To quote an American study, 'Professional development for teachers is essential to excellence, is vastly more costly than most people understand, and is flagrantly underfunded in most school improvement initiatives'.[14] Devolvement from the centre has proved damaging, because neither local authorities 'shopping around' institutions for cut-price courses nor making everything school-based because it is cheaper, is adequate. The axing of Area Training Organizations meant that there is now no place where the Inspectorate, the authorities, teachers and colleges and universities can plan coherently. We were interested that so many teachers referred nostalgically to DES/regional courses in English. Informally if not formally we urgently need to replace a wasteful system whereby institutions, groups and self-appointed 'consultants' make overlapping bids for custom, spending money and energy on competitive marketing, with one that empowers English teachers with full information about the possibilities open to them. If delegation is to be the norm, then instead of schools running unpopular and expensive 'whole-school' training on generalized topics, INSET budgets (now amounting to £600 per teacher annually, according to the government) should be devolved still further to subject departments. Consortia of school English departments, working with advisers and the appropriate staff from colleges and universities, could provide better and more wide-ranging planning groups than any single school can offer.

• Lastly, after years of successive ministerial innovations in education, few of them thought through before being launched, it is perhaps time for a period of what our doctor calls 'masterly inactivity' by government. The prevailing note of crisis management throughout schools and higher education, in which the agenda and terms of reference are always externally imposed, has exhausted teachers and taken attention away from teaching. Out-of-school activities with children, in which English teachers used to be vigorously engaged, have withered under pressure. In schools and in teacher education, as policy-making is more and more centralized, variety and ambiguity are tolerated less, and complex issues are over-simplified. Simultaneously, demands that institutions should all produce 'management plans' and 'financial projections' mean that teachers' time and energy for alternative issues are reduced or even eliminated. Over a decade the government has attacked standards in schools and in teacher education as a justification for pushing through (largely unresearched) revolutionary changes. Now we need time to see whether the results are any better; a period of stability to concentrate again on the teacher's real work.

As we have implied in that final point, beneath all the rhetoric, the thrust of the last decade has been to suggest that teachers are not really to be trusted. Their work must be regulated, appraised and inspected; they must be told what to teach and assessed on the success of their pupils; they and their schools must be made to compete with one another, as though education was a purchasable commodity like fish-fingers. Our response is simply to say that this should not be so, and that it is an ineffective policy. The evidence from our successful teachers is that they are driven much more effectively by their own professionalism than by any external forces. Poor teachers easily learn to circumvent regulations; good teachers are hampered rather than helped by them. Changing people is a slow business, but it is the central function of education. The government cannot provide society with good English teachers by some stroke of legislation. As this book illustrates, the best that it can do is to provide the conditions in which English teachers can learn to make themselves. Not for the first time, we find that Margaret Meek has expressed this better than we can:

> Contrary to popular belief, teachers are made not born. They become expert as other experts do, by a progressive understanding of what they are about .... What all teachers need is the chance and the possibility to develop their understandings in the company of their professional peers and others whose expertise enhances their own. They need regular challenging encounters with new ideas, new pedagogies, new research, and other teachers. It takes money and it takes time, but nothing less will suffice ....[15]

Appendix: 'Teachers of English' Research Project Questionnaire

1 Age in years: please indicate: ....

2 Sex: circle one: Male   Female

3 Qualifications: please circle any of the following you hold:
   Teachers Certificate   PGCE
   BEd   Higher degree (English)
   BA (English)   Higher degree (Education)
   BA (other)   Other (please specify)
                                 ....

4 Experience: please describe your present post here, and then circle on the list below
   any of the institutions in which you have taught:
   Present post...
   I have previously taught in –
       primary school   middle school
       secondary school   tertiary/6th form college
       FE college   other (specify)

5 Number of years spent teaching full-time in school ....

6 Number of schools in which you have taught ....

7 Membership of English-related organizations: please name below any to which you
   belong or have belonged:
       current membership   previous membership

*In the two following questions, 8 and 9, please rate each item by circling the appropriate
number, ranging from 5 (very) to 1 (none)*

8 How important and helpful in your development as a teacher do you consider each of
   the following to have been?

	degree of importance				
	none	little	some	much	great
(a) academic subject study	1	2	3	4	5
(b) teacher training course	1	2	3	4	5
(c) professional tutors in school	1	2	3	4	5
(d) heads of department	1	2	3	4	5
(e) other English teachers	1	2	3	4	5
(f) English advisers	1	2	3	4	5
(g) in-service courses	1	2	3	4	5
(h) membership of NATE or other organizations	1	2	3	4	5
(i) further academic study	1	2	3	4	5
(j) books or articles	1	2	3	4	5

If you have rated (j) at 4 or 5, please name here any book(s) or article(s) that have been of particular importance to you:

9 When you began teaching, how effectively did you feel you had been prepared in each of the following respects?

	degree of effectiveness				
	none	little	some	much	great
(a) organizing/encouraging talking and listening	1	2	3	4	5
(b) organizing/encouraging drama	1	2	3	4	5
(c) encouraging and marking written work	1	2	3	4	5
(d) book selection	1	2	3	4	5
(e) classroom work with novels and stories	1	2	3	4	5
(f) encouraging poetry reading and writing	1	2	3	4	5
(g) aiding children's language development	1	2	3	4	5
(h) knowledge of English language structure	1	2	3	4	5
(i) ways of working with the media	1	2	3	4	5
(j) planning coherent programmes of work	1	2	3	4	5
(k) teaching across the whole ability range	1	2	3	4	5
(l) understanding children's development in English	1	2	3	4	5
(m) keeping records of children's progress	1	2	3	4	5
(n) preparing classes for assessment at 16+	1	2	3	4	5
(o) Advanced level teaching	1	2	3	4	5

(p)	classroom management and control	1	2	3	4	5
(q)	management of small-group work	1	2	3	4	5
(r)	working with children with special needs	1	2	3	4	5
(s)	teaching English in a multicultural society	1	2	3	4	5
(t)	non-sexist teaching	1	2	3	4	5
(u)	use of Information Technology in English	1	2	3	4	5
(v)	school library work	1	2	3	4	5

10 In view of your later experience, what would you say were the *major* omissions from your course of preparation for English teaching? Name up to three, putting the most important first:

In the remaining questions, please answer briefly in your own words in the spaces provided. Add further comments on a separate sheet if you wish.

11 In what ways has your view of the nature of English teaching changed (if at all) since you began teaching?

12 What do you see as the most urgent problems facing English teachers at the moment?

13 What do you anticipate will be the most important changes in English teaching over the next ten years?

14 In what ways (if any) do you think that English teachers as a group are different from teachers of other subjects?

15 What seem to you the essential qualifications for someone who is going to become an effective English teacher?

16 Ideally, how do you think teachers of English should be trained?

17 When people talk of a 'career' in English teaching, what do you see as the different stages (or 'rungs' in the 'ladder')?

18 If you had friends (or children) who were thinking of becoming English teachers now, what advice would you give them?

In the final group of questions, those currently teaching in school are asked to respond to numbers 19–23, and those who are no longer in school to numbers 24–28

19 In what respects do you think your English teaching now is most different from when you began?

20 What at present are the chief obstacles to being able to teach as you wish?

21 For your own development, what kinds of in-service course would you most welcome?

22 In what ways (if any) has your expertise as an English teacher been used in school outside the classroom?

23 If you were able to take up a different post in the future, what would it be? (Please be as specific as possible.)

Section for those no longer teaching English full-time in schools

24 What is your present position, and what were your chief motives in seeking it?

25 What, if anything, do you miss about the school teaching of English?

26 What do you feel that you have gained in your present post by comparison with teaching English in school?

27 If in your present position you are making a contribution to the teaching of English, how would you describe that contribution?

28 What sort of advice would you give to an English teacher contemplating applying for a post like your own?

Thank you very much for your help in completing this questionnaire. We would be grateful if you would return it to Dr Robert Protherough, School of Education, University of Hull, Hull, HU6 7RX.

Notes and references

Introduction

1 This point is developed at greater length in the chapter on 'English' in Wiegand, P. and Rayner, M. (1989). *Curriculum Progress 5 to 16*. London, Falmer Press, especially pp. 119–22.
2 NCTE (1961). *The National Interest and the Teaching of English*. Champaign, Ill., NCTE; and Gill, M. and Crocker, W.J. (1980). *English in Teacher Education*. Armidale, NSW, University of New England.
3 Taylor, W. (1985). 'The future for teacher education', in D. Hopkins and K. Reid (eds), *Rethinking Teacher Education*. London, Croom Helm, p. 249.
4 Becher, A. (1989). *Academic Tribes and Territories*. Milton Keynes, Open University Press, p. 179.
5 Doyle, B. (1989). *English and Englishness*. London, Routledge, p. 6.
6 Quisenberry, J.D. (1981). 'English teacher preparation: what's happening', *English Education* 13 (2): 71.
7 Protherough, R. (1989). *Students of English*. London, Routledge.

Chapter 1 Shaping the image of an English teacher

1 For a fuller account, see Protherough, R. (1989). 'English as a subject', in *Students of English*. London, Routledge.
2 Board of Education (1921). *The Teaching of English in England* (the Newbolt Report). London, HMSO, para. 51.
3 Sampson, G. (1921). *English for the English*. Cambridge, Cambridge University Press, p. 20.
4 Board of Education (1910). *The Teaching of English in Secondary Schools*. London, HMSO, para. 10.
5 *The Teaching of English in England*, para. 18.
6 Ball, S.J. (1982). 'Competition and conflict in the teaching of English; a socio-historical analysis', *Journal of Curriculum Studies* 14 (1): 1.
7 Lawson, J. (1965). 'The historical background', *Aspects of Education* 3: 14–28.
8 Dent, H.C. (1977). *The Training of Teachers in England and Wales 1800–1975*. Sevenoaks, Hodder and Stoughton, ch. 7.

9 Collins, J.C. (1887). 'Can English Literature be taught?', *The Nineteenth Century* 22: 658.
10 See *Students of English*, ch. 1 and works referred to there.
11 Smith, N. (1918). 'The place of literature in education', in A.C. Benson (ed.), *Cambridge Essays on Education*. Cambridge, Cambridge University Press, pp. 107–8.
12 Ibid., pp. 118–9.
13 Protherough, R. (1981). 'The figure of the teacher in English literature, 1740–1918'. PhD thesis, Hull University.
14 Jacob, A. (1930). *Seventeen*. London, Methuen, p. 130.
15 See for example, Doyle, B. (1989). *English and Englishness*. London, Routledge, ch. 1.
16 Such ideas still animated the *Spens Report* of 1938, with its view that English teaching could 'soften the distinctions which separate men and classes in later life' (para. 222).
17 DES (1988). *Report of the Committee of Inquiry into the Teaching of English Language*. London, HMSO, p. 7. Compare this with George Sampson's (1921) comment nearly 70 years earlier that 'it cannot be said that the place of English in education is clearly seen', *English for the English*. Cambridge, Cambridge University Press, p. 15.
18 Board of Education (1924). *Some Suggestions for the Teaching of English in Secondary Schools in England*. London, HMSO, paras 1 and 10.
19 Mathieson, M. (1975). *The Preachers of Culture*. London, Allen and Unwin.
20 *English for the English*, p. 11.
21 Cook, C. (1917). *The Play Way*. London, Heinemann.
22 Leavis, F.R. (1930). *Mass Civilization and Minority Culture*. Cambridge, Gordon Fraser.
23 Mulhern, F. (1979). *The Moment of 'Scrutiny'*. London, New Left Books.
24 *English and Englishness*, p. 4.
25 *English for the English*, p. 102.
26 Ibid., p. 36.
27 Ibid., p. 7.
28 Benson, A.C. (ed.) (1918). *Cambridge Essays in Education*. Cambridge, Cambridge University Press, p. 118.
29 *English for the English*, pp. 55–6.
30 *Some Suggestions for the Teaching of English in Secondary Schools in England*, paras 32 and 4.
31 Mason, W.H. (1964). 'Introduction' in *For Teachers of English*. Oxford, Blackwell.
32 DES (1975). *A Language for Life*. London, HMSO, and HMI (1979). *Aspects of Secondary Education in England*. London, HMSO.
33 *English for the English*, p. 2.
34 Ibid., p. 79.
35 *The Preachers of Culture*, p. 169.
36 Ibid., pp. 162 and 168. An American survey, summing up the findings of numerous research studies, confirms this emphasis on personal qualities (see Koziol, S.M. Jr (1981). 'Enhancing English teacher effectiveness through the arts', *English Education* 13 (3): 147–55.
37 Board of Education (1910). *The Teaching of English in Secondary Schools*. London, HMSO, para. 3.
38 Witkin, R. (1974). *The Intelligence of Feeling*. London, Heinemann, and more recently Stables, A. (1990). 'Differences between pupils from mixed and single-sex schools in their enjoyment of school subjects …', *Educational Review* 42 (3): 221–30.

39 Goodson, I. and Medway, P. (1990). *Bringing English to Order*. London, Falmer Press, p. vii.
40 Donald, J. (1989). In P. Brooker and P. Humm (eds), *Dialogue and Difference*. London, Routledge, p. 28.
41 Cox, B. (1990). Editorial, *Critical Quarterly* 32 (4): 2.
42 *Preachers of Culture*, p. 194.
43 O'Malley, R. (1947). 'The purpose of teaching English', *English in Schools* 2 (5): 72.
44 *Preachers of Culture*, p. 208.
45 *Bringing English to Order*, op. cit.
46 For example, *Re-reading English* (1982). *New Directions in English Teaching* (1982), *Changing English* (1984), *Rewriting English* (1985), *Broadening the Context: English and Cultural Studies* (1987), *Dialogue and Difference: English into the Nineties* (1989), *Bringing English to Order* (1990), *Thinking through English* (1990), *Exploding English* (1990).
47 Mulhern, F. (1987). 'Prospects for English', *The English Magazine* 19: 32.
48 DES (1989). *English for Ages 5 to 16*. London, HMSO, paras 2.20 and 2.27.
49 Davies, C. (1989). 'The conflicting subject philosophies of English', *British Journal of Educational Studies* 38 (4): 413.

Chapter 2   Making careers in English teaching

1 Board of Education (1938). *Report of the Consultative Committee on Secondary Education*. London, HMSO, p. 300.
2 Bergen, B. (1982). 'Only a schoolmaster: gender, class and the effort to professionalize elementary teaching in England, 1870–1910', *History of Education Quarterly* 22: 1–21.
3 Apple, M.W. (1987). 'Gendered teaching, gendered labor', in T.S. Popkewitz (ed.), *Critical Studies in Teacher Education*. London, Falmer Press, pp. 57–83.
4 University Grants Committee (annual). *University Statistics*, Universities Statistical Record.
5 Acker, S. (1984). In S. Acker and D.W. Piper (eds), *Is Higher Education Fair to Women?* Guildford, SRHE and NFER Nelson, p. 36.
6 Board of Education (1923). *Consultative Committee on the Differentiation of the Curriculum for Boys and Girls Respectively in Secondary Schools*. London, HMSO.
7 Protherough, R. (1989). *Students of English*. London, Routledge, pp. 41–4, and DES (1989). *Statistics of Education*. London, HMSO.
8 Becher, A. (1989). *Academic Tribes and Territories*. Milton Keynes, Open University Press.
9 Lanier, J.E. and Little, J.W. (1986). 'Research on teacher education', in M.C. Wittrock (ed.), *The Handbook of Research on Teaching* (3rd edn.). New York, Macmillan, p. 561.
10 Roscoe, F. (1918). 'Teaching as a profession', in A.C. Benson (ed.), *Cambridge Essays on Education*. Cambridge, Cambridge University Press, p. 232.
11 Ginsburg, M. (1987). 'Reproduction, contradiction and conceptions of professionalism', in T.S. Popkewitz (ed.), *Critical Studies in Teacher Education*. London, Falmer Press, pp. 86–129.
12 Marr, A.L and MacLure, M. (forthcoming). *Teachers' Jobs and Lives*. ESRC, 1987–9.
13 *The Guardian*, 18 March 1968 and 25 September 1967.

14 *Times Educational Supplement*, 2 March and 29 June 1973, 28 March 1975; *The Guardian*, 8 November 1976; *Times Educational Supplement*, 28 January 1977.
15 *Sunday Times*, 30 August 1970.
16 *Times Educational Supplement*, 18 January 1974.
17 *Times Educational Supplement*, 28 November 1975.
18 *Times Educational Supplement*, 9 June 1978; *The Guardian*, 6 December 1978.
19 *Times Educational Supplement*, 24 May 1985, 20 January 1984, 5 July 1985, 26 July 1985, 18 July 1986, 28 November 1986.
20 *Times Educational Supplement*, 21 May 1989.
21 *The Guardian*, 6 December 1988.
22 *The Guardian*, 16 June 1988.
23 *The Guardian*, 7 November 1989 and 29 December 1989; *Times Educational Supplement*, 11 May 1990.
24 *The Guardian*, 6 November 1989; *Times Educational Supplement*, 3 March and 10 November 1989; HMI (1989). *Report on University of Oxford, Department of Educational Studies, Initial Teacher Training*. London, HMSO, para. 70.
25 HMI (1990). *A Survey of English in the Secondary Schools of Wales*. Cardiff, Welsh Office Education Department.

Chapter 3   The preparation of English teachers

1 *Times Educational Supplement*, 7 December 1990; Edwards, A. (1990). 'Schools of Education – their work and their future,' in J.B. Thomas (ed.), *British Universities and Teacher Education: A Century of Change*. London, Falmer Press, p. 180.
2 Board of Education (1924). *Some Suggestions for the Teaching of English in Secondary Schools in England*. London, HMSO, para. 1.
3 Board of Education (1921). *The Teaching of English in England* (the Newbolt Report). London, HMSO, paras 186–9.
4 Grommon, A.H. (1968). 'A history of the preparation of teachers of English', *English Journal* 57: 494.
5 Hosic, J.F. (1917). *Reorganization of English in Secondary Schools*. Bulletin No. 2, Washington DC, US Office of Education, p. 28.
6 HMI (1988). *The New Teacher in School*. London, HMSO, para. 1.19.
7 See for example, Robins, P. (1989). 'Actor training by degrees', MA dissertation. London, City University.
8 Mathieson, M. (1975). *The Preachers of Culture*. London, Allen and Unwin, pp. 175–9.
9 Taylor, W. (1969). *Society and the Education of Teachers*. London, Faber, p. 204.
10 Evans, C. (1988). *Language People*. Milton Keynes, Open University Press, pp. 106 and 110.
11 Ibid., p. 108.
12 Ibid., p. 108.
13 Moberly, W. (1949). *The Crisis in the University*. London, SCM Press, p. 251.
14 *Language People*, pp. 114–5 and Protherough, R. (1989). *Students of English*. London, Routledge, ch. 5.
15 Becher, A. (1989). *Academic Tribes and Territories*. Milton Keynes, Open University Press.
16 Ibid., p. 164.

17 Fuller, F. and Bown, O. (1975). 'Becoming a teacher', in K. Ryan (ed.), *Teacher Education*, 74th Yearbook of the National Society for the Study of Education. Chicago, Ill., Chicago University Press.
18 See Reid, K. (1985). *Rethinking Teacher Education*. London, Croom Helm, especially pp. 25–33; and Protherough, R. (1984). 'The quest for quality', *The Gadfly* 7 (1): 29–32.
19 *Times Educational Supplement*, 2 June 1989 and 30 November 1990.
20 HMI report, cited in *Times Educational Supplement*, 1 December 1989.

Chapter 4   How might English teachers be made?

1 *The Times*, 26 December 1990.
2 HMI (1988). *The New Teacher in School*. London, HMSO, para. 3.15.
3 Hoyle, E. (1974). 'Professionality, professionalism and control in teaching', *London Educational Review* 3 (2).
4 Heading for article by Rhodes Boyson, *The Observer*, 25 February 1990.
5 *Times Educational Supplement*, 8 September 1990. Professor Hargreaves has written a more reasoned and less journalistic paper in *Westminster Studies in Education* 13: 5–11 (1990), and we would agree with some of the points made there.
6 Mary Warnock in the *Times Educational Supplement*, 21 September 1990. See also her book (1988), *A Common Policy for Education*. Oxford, Oxford University Press, pp. 125–33.
7 *Times Educational Supplement*, 8 September, 1990.
8 Rae, J. (1990) 'Teachers set a bad example', *The Guardian*, 3 April.
9 Atkinson, J. (1989). 'How schools supervise students in training', in N. George and R. Protherough (eds), *Supervision in Education*. Hull University, pp. 28–34. See also Blake, D. (1990). 'The changing relationship between teachers and teacher educators: a case study', *British Journal of in-service Education* 16 (2): 86–90.
10 Swanwick K. and Chitty, C. (1989). 'Teacher education and the PGCE', cited in the *Times Educational Supplement*, 4 August.
11 *The New Teacher in School*, op. cit.
12 Harrison, B.T. *et al.* (1990). 'Framework and process in teaching practice', *Educational Review* 42 (3): 247; Atkinson (1989) op. cit. and the Australian works cited by Adams in ch. 5, n.15.
13 The Hillgate Group (1989). *Learning to Teach*. London, Claridge Press.
14 *Times Educational Supplement*, 7 December 1990 and 30 March 1990.
15 Lawlor, S. (1990). *Teachers Mistaught*. London, Centre for Policy Studies.
16 Quotations from: O'Hear, A. (1988). *Who Teaches the Teachers?* London, Social Affairs Unit, p. 21; The Hillgate Group (1989), op. cit., p. 11; Cox, C. *et al.* (1987). *The Reform of British Education*. London, Claridge Press, p. 36.
17 *Learning to Teach*, p. 8; *Who Teaches the Teachers?*, p. 6.
18 Protherough, R. (1989). *Students of English*. London, Routledge, chs 4 and 5.
19 *The Guardian*, 11 December 1990.
20 *The Reform of British Education*, p. 36.
21 *Who Teaches the Teachers?*, pp. 6 and 23; *Learning to Teach*, p. 5.
22 O'Keeffe, D. (1990). *The Wayward Elite*. London, Adam Smith Institute.
23 *The Guardian*, 2 March 1990.
24 Speech to the North of England Education Conference, 1989.

25 *Learning to Teach*, pp. 3–4.
26 HMI (1988). *Initial Teacher Training in Universities in England, Northern Ireland and Wales.* London, DES, p. 42.
27 *Learning to Teach*, pp. 1 and 4.
28 *The Reform of British Education*, p. 36.
29 *Who Teaches the Teachers?*, p. 27.
30 Benson, A.C. (ed.) (1918). *Cambridge Essays on Education.* Cambridge, Cambridge University Press, p. 218.
31 *The Guardian*, 25 February 1990.
32 Wilkinson, A. (1989). 'The supervision of higher degrees in education', in N. George and R. Protherough (eds), *Supervision in Education*. Hull University, pp. 45–6.

Chapter 5   Innovation in initial teacher education: the case of the PGCE

1 *Times Educational Supplement*, commencing 8 September 1989.
2 Hargreaves, D. (1989). 'Looking at a model of health', *Times Educational Supplement*, 1 December.
3 Adams, A. and Tulasiewicz, W. (1989). 'Which way the PGCE', *Times Educational Supplement*, 13 October.
4 Adams, A. (1970). 'On the education of teachers', in A. Adams (ed.), *Team Teaching and the Teaching of English*. Oxford, Pergamon, pp. 184–96.
5 Adams, A. (1989). 'And gladly teach: the English mother-tongue curriculum', in W. Tulasiewicz and A. Adams (eds), *Teachers' Expectations and Teaching Reality*. London, Routledge, pp. 117–32.
6 Lawlor, S. (1990). *Teachers Mistaught*. London, Centre for Policy Studies. This publication will give some indication of the kind of thinking involved.
7 An early but still thought-inspiring example of this dichotomy is to be found in this book by a retired HMI, Holmes, E. (1911). *What is and What might be*. London, Constable.
8 These issues are discussed by Anthony Adams and Witold Tulasiewicz in the *Times Educational Supplement*, commencing 21 September 1989.
9 DES (1984). *Teaching Quality*. Circular 3/84. London, HMSO. This was the original document that led in the 1980s to a wholesale overhaul of initial teacher education courses and to the establishment of CATE.
10 Adams, A. and Hadley, E. (1989). 'A study in method', in A. Adams (ed.), *New Directions in English Teaching*. London, Falmer Press.
11 Creber, J.W.P. (1990). *Thinking Through English*. Milton Keynes, Open University Press. This book provides a useful retrospective on some of the achievements in English teaching that characterized the 1960s.
12 Adams, A. (1990). 'The potential of information technology within the English Curriculum', *Journal of Computer Assisted Learning*, 6: 232–8. The full implications for IT of the Orders in Council for English in the National Curriculum are discussed in this paper.
13 Much of the work described here owes a great deal to the inspiration and experience of Brent Robinson.
14 Adams and Hadley (1989) op. cit.
15 A 'modem' is a simple piece of apparatus that links a computer to a telephone line so that messages, usually word-processed, can be sent from one microcomputer to

another via a 'host' mainframe computer. The whole process is generally known as
Electronic Mailing.

16 The occasional publication of the Microelectronics Education Support Unit (MESU)
entitled *Communique*, published through the Science Park at the University of
Warwick, describes much of the work that has been going on from 1989.

17 Adams, A. (1990). 'Distance support for student writing through electronic mailing',
Australian Journal of Remedial Education 22 (3): 28–31. This paper describes some
of the implications of this work for mixed ability English teaching.

18 Brent Robinson and others are preparing a book on some implications of electronic
communications for English teaching.

19 The Kingman Inquiry into the teaching of English language, reporting in 1988, made
a number of important recommendations for ITT and language teaching.

20 The Harris working group on the proposals for modern languages in the National
Curriculum has yet (1990) to present its report, but its recently published statement
of interim advice certainly envisages a place for knowledge about language as part of
the modern languages curriculum.

21 Turney, C. *et al.* (1985). *The Practicum Curriculum: A new Basis for Teacher
Education.* Sydney, Sydmac Academic Press. A helpful discussion of the 'triad'
and related ideas which have been developed in a number of universities in Australia.
I am grateful to Dr David Carter of the University of Western Australia for the
benefit of much helpful discussion on the matters raised here.

Chapter 6   English in the Oxford internship scheme

1 McIntyre, D. (1990). 'Ideas and principles guiding the Internship scheme', in P.
Benton (ed.), *The Oxford Internship Scheme.* London, Calouste Gulbenkian Foundation.

2 Benton, P. (ed.) (1990). op. cit.

3 Brighouse, T. (1990). 'The LEA engagement', in P. Benton (ed.), op. cit, pp. 123–33.

4 Ibid., p. 131.

5 Taken from documentation circulated to all mentors, curriculum tutors, general tutors
and professional tutors in the scheme, as *Briefing Papers for Professional Tutors and
Mentors*, OUDES (1990) (unpublished), section R1, point (iv).

6 Ibid., section R1, point (i).

Chapter 7   Promoting reflective teaching: a Scottish perspective

1 See, for example, Peacock, C. and Roger, A. (1984). *Success in Writing: a Classroom
Study with Slower Learning Pupils in Three Scottish Secondary Schools.* Dundee,
Scottish Consultative Council on the Curriculum; Peacock, C. (1986). *Teaching
Writing: A Systematic Approach.* Beckenham, Croom Helm.

2 For example, Morrison, A. and McIntyre, D. (1973). *Teachers and Teaching* (2nd
edn.), Harmondsworth, Penguin; Dunkin, M.J. and Biddle, B.J. (1974). *The Study of
Teaching.* New York, Holt, Rinehart, Winston; Wragg, E.C. (ed.) (1984). *Classroom
Teaching Skills.* Beckenham, Croom Helm.

3 See Peacock, C. (1990). *Classroom skills in English teaching: a self-appraisal framework.*
London, Routledge.

4 See Gilmore, S. (1977). 'Microteaching and the professional education of teachers of

English', in D. McIntyre, G. MacLeod and R. Griffiths (eds), *Investigations of Microteaching*. Beckenham, Croom Helm, pp. 233–9.

5 See *Investigations of Microteaching*.

6 Butts, D. (1984). *A Concept of Partnership: An Evaluation of the Stirling Collaborative Project on Teacher Education*. Stirling Educational Monographs no. 12, University of Stirling.

7 See Peacock, C. (1990) op. cit., chs 2–5.

8 Scottish Education Department (1978). *Learning to Teach* (the Sneddon Report). Edinburgh, HMSO.

9 See Butts, D. (1984) op. cit., for an abridged version of the final report.

Chapter 8   English in the formation of primary teachers

1 Laing, R.D. (1970) *Knots*. Harmondsworth, Penguin.

2 Martin, N. (1983). *Mainly about Writing*. London, Heinemann.

3 Armstrong, M. (1987). *Times Educational Supplement*, 15 May.

4 Brook, P. (1968). *The Empty Space*. London, Macgibbon and Kee.

5 Milosz, C. (1980). 'Ars Poetica', in C. Milosz and L. Vallee (eds), *Bells in Winter*. Manchester, Carcanet.

Chapter 9   How English teachers make themselves

1 Becher, A. (1987). 'Disciplinary discourse', *Studies in Higher Education* 12 (3): 262.

2 The Board of Education (1921). *The Teaching of English in England* (the Newbolt Report). London, HMSO, para. 108.

3 See Protherough, R. (1986). *Teaching Literature for Examinations*. Milton Keynes, Open University Press, pp. 5–7.

4 See Shayer, D. (1972), *The Teaching of English in Schools 1900–1970*. London, Routledge, pp. 111–19 and elsewhere.

5 Taylor, W. (1985). 'The future for teacher education', in D. Hopkins and K. Reid (eds), *Rethinking Teacher Education*. London, Croom Helm, p. 244.

6 DES (1972). *Teacher Education and Training*. London, HMSO, para. 2.23.

7 Wragg, E. (1989). The *Times Higher Educational Supplement*, 17 November; based on returns from 29 universities, comparing 1988–9 with 1986–7: a drop from 2,112 to 320, exacerbated by a 60 per cent fall in the number of self-financed students.

8 Hart, R. (1990). *Times Educational Supplement*, 14 December.

9 Earley, P. and Fletcher-Campbell, F. (1989). 'The time to manage? Department and faculty heads at work', NFER research study, reported in the *Times Educational Supplement*, 20 October.

Chapter 10   Conclusion: Making it better

1 Hartog, P. (1947). *Words in Action*. London, University of London Press, chs 1 and 2.

2 Barnes, D. and Barnes, D. (1984). *Versions of English*. London, Heinemann, p. 215.

3 MacCabe, C. (1990). 'Language, literature, identity: reflections on the Cox Report', *Critical Quarterly* 32 (4): 7.

4 See Shayer, D. (1972). *The Teaching of English in Schools 1900–1970*. London, Routledge and Kegan Paul, pp. 86–92.

5 Wideen, M.F. (1985). 'Characteristics of faculties of education', in D. Hopkins and K. Reid, *Rethinking Teacher Education*. Beckenham, Croom Helm, pp. 83–106. Compare David Hopkins in the same volume.

6 See Henry, G.H. (1986). 'What is the nature of English education?', *English Education* 18 (1): 4–41.

7 See Farrell, E.J. (1983). 'English education: a time for new models and measures', *English Education* 15 (4): 231–8.

8 Olson, M.C. (1982). 'Our profession and the popular wisdom', *English Education* 14 (3): 157–60.

9 *Times Educational Supplement*, 7 December 1990.

10 HMI (1988). *The New Teacher in School*. London, HMSO, para. 1.41.

11 Protherough, R. (1989). *Students of English*. London, Routledge, pp. 178–84.

12 Marr, A.L. and MacLure, M. (forthcoming). *Teachers' Jobs and Lives*. ESRC, 1987–9.

13 We are indebted to Michael Saunders, of Nottingham University, for drawing this to our attention.

14 Gray, D. (1985). *Basic Education* 30 (1): 4.

15 Meek, M. (1985). In Slater F. (ed.), *The Quality Controllers*. London, London University Institute of Education (Bedford Way papers no. 22), p. 27.

Index